# WHO ARE YA?

# WHO ARE
# YA?

The **talkSPORT** Book of
**Football's Best Ever Chants**

Gershon Portnoi

**SIMON &
SCHUSTER**

London · New York · Sydney · Toronto · New Delhi

A CBS COMPANY

First published in Great Britain
by Simon & Schuster UK Ltd, 2011
A CBS Company

3 5 7 9 10 8 6 4 2

Simon & Schuster UK Ltd
1st Floor
222 Gray's Inn Road
London
WC1X 8HB

**www.simonandschuster.co.uk**

Simon & Schuster Australia
Sydney

Simon & Schuster India
New Delhi

A CIP catalogue for this book is available
from the British Library.

ISBN: 978-0-85720-668-8

Typeset and designed by
Craig Stevens and Julian Flanders

Printed and bound in Great Britain
by Butler Tanner & Dennis
Somerset
BA11 1NF

# Contents

# ::: INTRODUCTION

About six months ago I was minding my own business while travelling on the London Underground. Although I have on-trend dark brown curly hair which can sometimes get mistaken for an eighties footballer's perm, I tend not to stick out too much on public transport. A group of 'city boys' alongside me were sniggering and they suddenly burst into song:

> Oh Christian Dailly,
> You are the love of my life,
> Oh Christian Dailly,
> I'd let you shag my wife,
> Oh Christian Dailly,
> You've got curly hair too!

The penny dropped. The lads were West Ham fans, who evidently believed that I resembled their former perm-haired central defensive hero. It wasn't the time or the place to argue with them that they were wrong – I clearly looked much more like Kevin Keegan – because I suddenly had the inspiration to collate the funniest, wittiest and most unusual football chants into a book, which hopefully you have just purchased. (If you're just standing in a shop reading this, walk to the till right now and pay for it. I have a family to support.)

This collection isn't meant to be comprehensive. There aren't enough trees in the country to provide paper for every song that's ever been sung at a British football ground. Instead, this book is jam-packed with a selection of the best chants and details of their origins.

All football chants directed at opponents are essentially designed to get under the skin of either the fans, manager, players, owner or even the physio of the other team. (And also the officials too.) The best are funny, some are interesting and a few are hugely controversial. But everything within a chant, including truth and fairness, is sacrificed to wit. Indeed the most unfair chants are sometimes the funniest. Fans jump at the chance to falsely accuse if it makes for a good song.

As well as exploring (OK, laughing at) all these chants, I've taken a cultural and historical look at the evolution of chanting in this country, which to my mind has the funniest and most intelligent football fans in the world. This book is really a celebration of a positive side of our fan culture, of which we should be proud. And just to show we're not too insular, there's an amusing look at what fans in other countries sing while they watch their football.

To help your enjoyment of the book, there's a little key below to explain the tunes of the majority of the chants so that they make sense and so that you can sing along in your head while you're reading.

**Gershon Portnoi**
London, July 2011

# ▦ CHANT TUNE KEY

'Cwm Rhondda' ('Bread of Heaven')
The tune for thousands of football chants from 'You're not singing anymore' to 'Shall we sing a song for you?'

'Go West'
Ubiquitous tune for chants ranging from 'One-nil to the Arsenal' to 'You're shit and you know you are'.

'Quartermaster's Store'
Usually used for singing about particular players like 'He's fat, he's round, he bounces on the ground ...'

'Volare'
Made popular by Arsenal's chant for Patrick Vieira: 'Vieira, woah-oh'.

'Lord of the Dance'
Still widely used, most famously by Chelsea: 'Carefree, wherever we may be ...'

'Tom Hark'
The Piranhas song is the tune for 'Champions League, you're having a laugh' and many more.

'Guantanamera'
The inspiration behind a huge number of chants from 'There's only one ...' to 'Sing when you're winning'.

'Son of My Father'
Not as popular as it used to be, most famously used for songs about Teddy Sheringham like 'Oh Teddy Teddy ...'

'When Johnny Comes Marching Home Again'
Currently doing the rounds as it was used for Liverpool's Fernando Torres song and many others.

'Stars and Stripes Forever'
The tune for 'Here we go' and lots more which just use a team name e.g. 'Newcastle, Newcastle, Newcastle'.

# ALAN BRAZIL

**Despite a playing career that took the Scottish striker to Ipswich, Spurs, Man United and even Australia, it's little surprise that when it comes to chants Alan Brazil can look no further than Celtic.** Having grown up in Glasgow and escaped home to sneak into games at Parkhead when he was a child, Celtic has always been close to Brazil's heart.

And although Liverpool fans were first to sing 'You'll Never Walk Alone' as an anthem, it quickly became a huge chant at Celtic, where the supporters also raise their green-and-white-hooped scarves and sing in unison before kick-off – something that appealed to Brazil from a very young age: 'I love "You'll Never Walk Alone" because of the way it is sung ahead of games at Celtic Park,' he says. 'There's nothing like it, it's so stirring when the whole crowd sing it together as the teams are about to come out.'

> When you walk through a storm,
> Hold your head up high,
> And don't be afraid of the dark
> At the end of the storm,
> Is a golden sky,
> And the sweet silver song of the lark
> Walk on through the wind,
> Walk on through the rain,
> Though your dreams be tossed and blown
> Walk on, walk on, with hope in your heart,
> And you'll never walk alone,
> You'll never walk alone

Alan Brazil made no secret of how many bottles of Champagne he'd be drinking after the game.

# 1

## 'THERE'S ONLY ONE ...'

**M**ost football chants are derivative. We sing the same tunes, slightly adjust the words and, hey presto, a new terrace anthem is born. But there are some chants that will always be unique. It's not so much that they can't be repeated, for nothing is sacred – especially in the stands – but it's more due to their original nature. In this chapter, we salute the most inspired pieces of lyrical invention ever to grace a football stadium.

# ::: SEEING DOUBLE

There can only ever have been one football chant written specifically for two different players and Man United sing it. Young Brazilian twin full backs Rafael and Fabio Da Silva have become cult figures at Old Trafford with a series of dazzling displays since breaking into the first team in 2008/09 at the age of 18.

However, the twins are identical and most United fans have little idea how to tell them apart, hence the following chant which is sung to the continental tune of Roma's 'Forza Roma':

> Viva Da Silva,
> Viva Da Silva,
> Running down the pitch,
> Don't know which is which,
> Viva Da Silva!

The Da Silvas' synchronised defending routine failed to impress the *Britain's Got Talent* judges.

## ▦ O'BRIENS' DOUBLE ACT

Newcastle have a similar chant although their two players merely have the same surname but are not related, nor do they look alike. In fact, they weren't even on the club's books at the same time.

However, Liam O'Brien and Andy O'Brien both shared the distinction of scoring for the Toon against arch-rivals Sunderland. To celebrate this fact, the Geordie fans concocted a wonderfully original chant to the tune of 'Any Old Iron':

> Liam O'Brien, Andy O'Brien,
> Any, any, any O'Brien,
> Who put the ball in the Mackems' net?
> O'Brien, O'Brien!

## ▦ POLITICALLY INCORRECT

Celtic's Japanese star Shunsuke Nakamura must have been surprised at the chant that was composed in his honour following his arrival at Parkhead. If he didn't know about the complicated political situation in Glasgow before his arrival, he would certainly have been educated by the Bhoys fans chant about him. The fact that they sang about a popular Chinese dish for a Japanese player can be glossed over; such is the humour and originality behind this effort to 'Winter Wonderland':

> There's only one Nakamura,
> There's only one Nakamura,
> He eats Chow Mein,
> He votes Sinn Fein,
> Walking in a Naka wonderland!

## ▦ HEALY'S SECOND COMING

Many supporters have chanted the traditional Christmas hymn 'Away in a Manger' to have a pop at their rivals. Usually, the chant is adapted to 'the little lord Jesus looked up and he said' followed by 'we hate' and the insertion of a rival team's name.

Northern Ireland fans managed to produce a bespoke version of this song by continuing with the original words of the hymn until the line 'the stars in the bright sky looked down where he lay'. At this point, their worship of striker David Healy got the better of their love for Jesus:

Away in a manger,
No crib for a bed,
The little lord Jesus lay down his sweet head,
The stars in the bright sky looked down where...
Healy!
Healy!
Healy!
Healy!

## ▦ FAHEY'S FELLOWSHIP

There was similar wordplay at work from Birmingham City fans who composed a witty chant for their own Keith Fahey. Using the traditional song from birthday parties, Blues fans sung the following:

Fahey's a jolly good fellow,
Fahey's a jolly good fellow,
Fahey's a jolly good fellow,
And so say all of us!

## ▦ FROM RUSSIA WITH LOVE

In these days of multicultural Premier League football where English teams are made up of talent from all four corners of the globe, names are not what they used to be. Some surnames do not lend themselves to chants, a case in point being Everton's Russian midfielder Diniyar Bilyaletdinov. But that didn't stop some Goodison Park wags coming up with the following song to the tune of 'Quartermaster's Store':

He's quick,
He's game,
We can't pronounce his name,
Russian lad, Russian lad!

## ▦ DIOUF'S SPITTING IMAGE

El-Hadji Diouf is a footballer with a reputation for being unconventional.
No stranger to controversy, the Senegalese striker is a player fans love to hate
and the feeling is mutual as he has twice spat at opposition supporters,
landing himself (and them) in hot water. It was little surprise that Bolton
fans composed the following chant for him to the tune of 'Is This the Way
to Amarillo?':

Sha la la la la la la la
Diouf Diouf!
Sha la la la la la la la
Diouf Diouf!
Sha la la la la la la la
Diouf Diouf!
El-Hadji Diouf will spit on you!

## ▦ ROMAN EARNS HIS SPURS

The days when football fans only had to remember one, or at a push, two
words to chant from the terraces are long gone and Tottenham's loyal
followers proved that with their ode to Roman Pavlyuchenko.

The Russian striker took a while to settle in at White Hart Lane, but
eventually hit a rich vein of form that led to a fitting tribute that played
to his eastern European stereotype. Chanted to the unlikely tune of
'Supercalifragilistic' from *Mary Poppins*, Spurs sang:

Even with his team-mate's help the big-headed Russian couldn't squeeze into his shirt.

Supercalifragilistic Roman Pavlyuchenko,
Tottenham Hotspur's number 9 is better than Shevchenko,
Like all Russians, always has a vodka in his Kenco,
Supercalifragilistic Roman Pavlyuchenko

## ::::: BREDE OF FULHAM

With owner Mohammad al-Fayed having erected a statue of Michael Jackson outside Craven Cottage, Fulham are hardly famous for football culture, but that didn't stop their embarrassed fans coming up with a superb tribute to their Norwegian centre-back Brede (pronounced Brayder) Hangeland.

Plucked from as close to obscurity as is possible in the modern game by Roy Hodgson, Hangeland's majestic performances at the heart of Fulham's defence soon earned him rave reviews. And the west London club's supporters did his displays justice with the following song, to the tune of Bread of Heaven:

(It's worth noting that the original lyrics of this Welsh favourite are: 'Bread of heaven, bread of heaven, feed me till I want no more'.)

Brede Hangeland,
Brede Hangeland,
He is Norway's Bobby Moore!

# ▦ GETTING ON CITY'S GOAT

Manchester City fans also famously made use of the 'Bread of Heaven' tune with their song for goalscoring cult hero Shaun Goater. With the club at their lowest ebb after plummeting to the third tier of English football for the first time, Goater provided the spark that set City on the road to recovery. Over five seasons, the Bermudan netted more than 100 times as City returned to the top flight. For every goal and every game, the die-hard fans serenaded him with the subsequent simple truth which Plato himself could not have put any better:

Feed the goat and he will score

# ▦ ARSENAL'S HLEB OF DECEIT

Having started the craze for chants based on the Pet Shop Boys' 'Go West' with their 'One-nil to the Arsenal', the Gooners also laid claim to launching songs inspired by the much-covered hit 'Volare'. With their classic tribute to their inspirational captain Patrick Vieira ('He came from Senegal, to play for Ar-se-nal'), a host of spin-offs were soon doing the rounds.

But, it was the Emirates fans who managed to rip themselves off in the best and most original way with this ever-so-slightly xenophobic ditty about their Belorussian midfielder Alexander Hleb:

Alex Hleb, woah-oh,
Alex Hleb, woah-oh,
He came from Belarus
To sell cheap fags and booze

# ▦ ORIENT MEMBERS SING UP

A classic chant that rival fans used to sing to each other went along the lines of 'We'll go running round the (insert hated team here) with our willies hanging out; singing I've got a bigger one than you.' So it's hard to imagine any set of fans celebrating having inferior manhoods. Step forward, supporters of the mighty Leyton Orient.

Season 2010/11 was the club's best in three decades and the fans celebrated with a memorable song about new signing Dean Cox, a 5ft 4in former

Brighton winger who finished the campaign with 11 goals and 19 assists.

Not a bad return for the player known as 'Tiny' who was lauded as follows by the Brisbane Road faithful to the appropriately Cockney tune of 'Knees Up Mother Brown' (Albion first chanted the words to this song, but not the tune):

We've got Tiny Cox,
We've got Tiny Cox,
We've got Tiny
We've got Tiny
We've got Tiny Cox!

## ▦ OPERA AT SCUNTHORPE

There's not much that's more elitist in British society than the opera. So it's only fitting that a recently popular football chant has been based on one of the most famous operatic melodies of all time: 'La Donna è Mobile' from Verdi's *Rigoletto*.

This chant started doing the rounds at around about the same time as the foreign invasion of the Premier League. Sheffield Wednesday fans could be heard singing the name of their hero Paolo Di Canio to this tune and it spread like wildfire. But, without doubt, the greatest interpretation of this number came from the unlikely destination of Scunthorpe.

When Iron chairman Steve Wharton appointed the club's physiotherapist Nigel Adkins as caretaker manager following the departure of Brian Laws in November 2006, many people in football would have questioned his sanity. Yet, Adkins promptly guided United to the League One title and to a first appearance in the second tier for 40 years. The Glanford Park faithful paid tribute to Adkins in the best possible way:

Who needs Mourinho?
We've got our physio!

## ⸬ BURY'S HOME SHOPPING

Having seen a tricky one earlier in this chapter, some football surnames are akin to open goals for the terrace choirs. If you're lucky enough to have a striker with the surname Cole, for example, it doesn't take a great leap to arrive at a chant which rhymes his surname with 'goal'. But the task wasn't that straightforward for Bury fans when their teamsheet featured Lenny John-Lewis.

The double-barrelled name didn't really lend itself to a song but when the striker popped up with a late winner from the bench against Morecambe, the bards behind the goal at Gigg Lane celebrated with what is, without doubt, the only song of its kind in world football. And they used 'La Donna è Mobile' to do it justice:

> His name's a department store,
> You know he's gonna score!

## ⸬ IN THE NAME OF THE FATHER

It's not unusual for a fans' hero to have one or several chants composed for him by his loyal supporters. However, it is slightly out of the ordinary for that hero's parent to be sung about too. But the inhabitants of Liverpool's Kop are strong believers in identity and family and they reacted with typical Scouse humour in response to an unfortunate incident that saw Jamie Carragher's father banned from all UK football grounds.

Gary Carragher was ejected from Villa Park for allegedly being drunk during an England match in which his son was playing in 2005. He received bail from the court, but only on the condition that he was not allowed inside any UK football ground until the case was settled – a tough break for the man who rarely missed a game his son played.

It wasn't long before the following chant could be heard from the Liverpool masses to the tune of 'Quartermaster's Store':

> He's red,
> He's sound,
> He's banned from every ground,
> Carra's dad, Carra's dad!

## ▦ DEAR JOHN

In terms of lyrical wit and ingenuity, it's hard to believe that a finer, more original chant could have been conceived in football than this ode to Stern John. The burly Trinidadian striker became a hero at Nottingham Forest and Birmingham as much for his goalscoring prowess as for the cult chant which was started in his honour – the verses to which Noel Coward or even Oscar Wilde would have been proud to have penned.

Using the 'Quartermaster's Store' again, the fans chanted:

He's big,
He's fast,
His first name should come last,
Stern John, Stern John

## ▦ HARDCORE SUPPORT

A chant that has since been imitated by other supporters may seem a strange inclusion in a section full of unique offerings. But, at the time, Arsenal's tribute to ponytailed midfielder Emmanuel Petit was so distinct it has to be worthy of a mention.

The Frenchman's mercurial midfield displays helped galvanise Arsène Wenger's Gunners into an all-conquering Double-winning machine. Petit was the silent but effective type, full of Gallic charm and a World Cup-winner to boot. And Highbury's North Bank used 'Quartermaster's Store' to salute him thus:

He's blond,
He's slick,
His name's a porno flick,
Emmanuel, Emmanuel

Petit's pre-match warm-up was the stuff of legend.

## ▦ CITY'S PROTEST SONG

There are no shortage of original and witty Manchester City chants but in the interests of balance and fairness  only a couple can be featured in this chapter.

When the Blues endured their previously mentioned dark age in the third tier of English football, a chant began which is still sung to this very day – although for very different reasons. Some fans point to Macclesfield away as the moment the song first received an airing, but the consensus is that it was during the 1998/99 season.

The song, which is sung to the tune of 'We Shall Not Be Moved', describes the disbelief at the club's plight at the time. The fans continued to sing it for years after they came out of the doldrums and it was sung with renewed vigour when the club was bought by a billionaire Arab, who embarked on an unparalleled spending spree. There was disbelief on a different scale and when City won their first trophy for 35 years in the 2011 FA Cup final, Wembley was swaying to the sounds of 'We're Not Really Here':

> We are not, we're not really here
> We are not, we're not really here
> Just like the fans of the invisible man
> We're not really here

## ▦ A TALL TALE

Sometimes simple is best. Another witty Scouse effort was composed for Peter Crouch. The giant striker was perfect fodder for football chants. Standing at about 9ft 10in and internationally recognised as the world's thinnest, most awkward-looking character ever to set foot on a football pitch, each time Crouch runs, leading experts in medical science are left baffled at his coordination. It shouldn't be possible.

Yet, jokes aside, Crouch has scored goals wherever he has played and the Kop felt moved enough to sum up their one-time hero with this chant, once again to the tune of 'Quartermaster's Store' (it's a popular number in Liverpool):

> He's tall, he's Red,
> His feet stick out the bed,
> Peter Crouch, Peter Crouch

# ▦ ARSENAL GO FOR A SONG

Arsenal home fans are not known for their noise. Highbury used to be known as 'The Library' while the new Emirates Stadium is rarely described as atmospheric. Yet the loyal Gooners have managed to conjure up some of British football's most memorable chants.

One of the most popular songs opposing fans use to mock each other's poor support is: 'One song, you've only got one song' to the tune of 'Blue Moon'. And Arsenal fans managed to turn this to their advantage when they signed Cameroon international midfielder Alex Song:

> One Song,
> We've only got one Song!

# ▦ FC'S PC CHANT

Arsenal's poetry caught on, and the recently formed Man United protest club, FC United, who pride themselves on their chants, were soon singing 'We've only got one Tong' for their central defender Adam Tong. Formed in the wake of the Glazer takeover of Manchester United, FC fans are disillusioned Reds who wanted a return to grass roots football where supporters stand and sing their hearts out for their team without a prawn sandwich in sight.

As such, FC games are always lively affairs with a lot of noise generated. One of their favourite chants is reserved not for any particular player, manager or opponent but for the police. Whenever any members of the local constabulary walk past the gathered masses behind the goal, FC fans sing (to the tune of 'Sloop John B'):

> We paid for your hats,
> We paid for your hats,
> What a waste of council tax,
> We paid for your hats

# ▦ TOP OF THE POPS

The Scottish national team haven't had a great deal to cheer about over the years save Archie Gemmill's goal against Holland in the 1978 World Cup – a tournament for which England failed to qualify, another reason to be cheerful.

But the lack of success has never stopped the fans from north of the border following their team through thick and thin and having the best possible time on their travels. The Tartan Army normally travel in kilts and ginger wigs and are never far away from city centre bars. But, to the tune of 'Land of Hope and Glory', one of their best songs unusually celebrates soft drinks:

> We hate Coca-Cola,
> We hate Fanta too,
> We're the Tartan Army
> And we love Irn Bru!

The Tartan Army were at it again during an international in Italy although this time they'd probably consumed more than just Irn Bru. Warming to their hosts' hospitality, the Scotland fans used the 'Guantanamera' tune to chant:

> Deep fry your pizzas,
> We're gonna deep fry your pizzas!

# ▦ CHRISTMAS COMES EARLY
# AT BLACKBURN

As already noted, the arrival of foreign players in the UK – or 'Carlos Kickaballs' as former Spurs chairman Alan Sugar famously labelled them – also led to a variety of interesting surnames which encouraged greater creativity. This was illustrated perfectly when Blackburn Rovers signed Bayern Munich's Paraguay striker Roque Santa Cruz and welcomed him to their Ewood Park home by singing an abridged version of the old Christmas hit:

> Santa Cruz is coming to town,
> Santa Cruz is coming to town,
> Santa Cruz is coming, to town

## ▦ BIBLE BASHING AT THE PALACE

When they're not bopping along to 'Glad All Over' Crystal Palace fans clearly have a sense of humour, judging from a song for young striker Victor Moses. The Eagles handed a debut to the Nigerian-born local lad at the age of just 16 and he quickly became a cult hero for the Selhurst Park faithful. Going down the well-trodden path of the 'Volare' song, Palace's tribute went as follows:

> Oh Moses, woah-oh,
> Oh Moses, woah-oh,
> He comes from Norbury,
> He parted the Red Sea!

## ▦ OLDHAM'S CHEST JEST

It's fitting to end a section on unique chants with one that only fans of one club in the world could ever sing – in the words of Andy Gray 'take a bow' Oldham Athletic.

The chant gained popularity in the seventies, a time when political correctness was a term that would have meant as much to people as the internet. There's no explanation necessary and no tune, just genius wordplay:

> Give us a T (T),
> Give us an I (I),
> Give us a T (T),
> Give us an S (S),
> What do you do with 'em?
> Old-em!
> Old-em!

# JIMMY BULLARD

**Jimmy Bullard has enjoyed a diverse and highly successful career, ranging from appearing for Gravesend & Northfleet to turning out in the Premier League for Fulham and Hull.** Wherever the wavy-haired midfielder has played, he has brought joy to thousands.

'While I was on loan at Ipswich they used to sing a really funny song about me,' says Bullard. 'I used to take all the corners and free kicks. I went over to take a corner and I could clearly hear all the fans singing that I could shag their wives! I thought "I can shag their wives? That's a bit deep isn't it?" It really did make me laugh.' Here's the full version of the Ipswich fans' song, to the tune of 'Can't Take My Eyes Off You':

Oh Jimmy Bullard, you are the love of my life,
Oh Jimmy Bullard, I'd let you shag my wife,
Oh Jimmy Bullard, I want curly hair too!

Bullard couldn't hide his excitement at the long line of wives.

# DANCEFLOOR CHANTS

Increasingly, football fans have taken inspiration not from old tunes but from contemporary chart-based songs. This is nothing new, but what has changed is the ingenuity with which it's been done. Arsenal's 'One-nil to the Arsenal' was created in 1994 after the PA at Parc des Princes played the Pet Shop Boys' 'Go West' during half time, when the Gunners were beating Paris St Germain 1-0. This chapter celebrates some of the finest transitions from hit parade to kop hit.

## STIG OF THE GANG

As has been noted, the influx of international surnames to the Premier League has given fans many new avenues to explore in terms of their chanting creativity. Liverpool were at the forefront of this new poetry with their chant for Norwegian Stig Inge Bjornebye, to the tune of Gary Glitter's 'I'm the Leader of the Gang':

> Bjornebye in my gang, my gang, my gang,
> Bjornebye in my gang, oh yeah!
> Bjornebye in my gang, my gang, my gang,
> Bjornebye in my gang, oh yeah!
> Stig Inge, Stig Inge, Stig Inge Bjornebye!
> Stig Inge, Stig Inge, Stig Inge Bjornebye!

## LEEDS UNITED DO THE KAISER CHIEFS

Since the glory days of the seventies and the unforgettable run to the Champions League semi-finals in 2000, Leeds fans could be forgiven for taking a more gloomy outlook on life. But, despite the club having spent several seasons in the third tier of English football, its supporters retained a sense of humour throughout. However, in the 2006/07 season, with the club's form both home and away having improved dramatically due to the drop in level at which they were playing, the faithful emerged with a belter based on local band Kaiser Chiefs' 2005 top ten hit 'Oh My God!'

The chorus sung by the chart-toppers was 'Oh my god, I can't believe it, I've never been this far away from home,' but, when they were on their way to another three points on their travels, the Leeds fans chanted:

> Oh my god, I can't believe it,
> We've never been this good away from home!

## PALACE GO DIVA

In what must surely be the only recorded history of a football chant based on a Whitney Houston song, Crystal Palace fans used their imagination to serenade their French signing Alassane N'Diaye. He may not have made such a big impact on the pitch, other than scoring two goals in a week soon after his debut, but the temptation of playing with his surname was too hard to resist for some fans. And resist they could not as Eagles supporters cleverly adapted (without actually changing any of the words) Houston's mega-hit 'I Will Always Love You' for their new hero by simply singing:

> N'Diayeeeee, will always love you!

## ▦ LIVERPOOL BLAME IT ON TRAORE

It's not often that fans compose chants to mock their own players but Liverpool supporters just couldn't abide any more of defender Djimi Traore's performances. At a time when the club was longing for a return to its glory years of dominating English football, the frustration was just too much for some Anfield regulars who came up with an instant classic to pin all the team's troubles on poor Traore. Harsh but hilarious.

Using The Jackson Five's 'Blame it on the Boogie' for inspiration, and blessed with the good fortune of having several squad members who had rhyming surnames, they came up with a highly original alternative to the famous lyrics: 'Don't blame it on the sunshine, don't blame it on the moonlight, don't blame it on the good times, blame it on the boogie. I just can't, I just can't, I just can't control my feet':

> Don't blame it on the Biscan,
> Don't blame it on the Hamann,
> Don't blame it on the Finnan,
> Blame it on Traore.
> He just can't, he just can't, he just can't control his feet.

## ▦ ARSENAL TALK ABOUT CESC

At around the same time as Traore's humiliation, a star was being born in north London and Arsenal fans produced a similarly inspired version of Salt-n-Pepa's 1991 hit 'Let's Talk About Sex' to hail young Cesc Fabregas.

Like Liverpool's Jacksons rip-off, the original lyrics must be studied to appreciate the subtle nuances and updates in the Gunners' song. 'Let's talk about sex baby, let's talk about you and me, let's talk about all the good things and the bad things that we see, let's talk about sex.' Making the leap from 'sex' to 'Cesc' was hardly a challenge, but the rest is pure poetry:

> Let's talk about Cesc baby,
> Let's talk about Fla-min-I,
> Let's talk about Theo Walcott, Freddie Ljungberg and Henry,
> Let's talk about Cesc!

## ▥ CITY'S OASIS TRIBUTE

It was inevitable that as soon as Man City supporting brothers Noel and Liam Gallagher shot to fame with Oasis that the long-suffering fans of the club would adopt at least one of the band's anthems as their own.

Often seen at matches together, before their very public falling out, the Gallaghers' 'Roll With It' quickly became the tune to welcome the teams

Kinkladze's 'Invisible Man' power always foxed the opposition.

emerging from the tunnel. But it was 'Wonderwall' that became the anthem of choice for the club's loyal followers, who used it to pay tribute to their struggling 1995/96 relegation-bound side, which featured the mercurial skills of Georgie Kinkladze under the stewardship of Alan Ball.

The Oasis original featured the verses and chorus: 'And all the roads that lead us there are winding; and all the lights that light the way are blinding; there are many things that I would like to say to you but I don't know how. Because maybe you're gonna be the one that saves me; and after all, you're my wonderwall.' It only took a slight tweak to the Gallaghers' version before the following could be heard ringing around Maine Road:

> And all the runs that Kinky makes are winding,
> And all the goals that City score are blinding,
> There are many times that we would like to score again
> But we don't know how.
> 'Cos maybe, you're gonna be the one that saves me,
> And after all, you're my Alan Ball

## UNITED'S LACK OF CITY PITY

City's plight at the time they dropped out of the top flight and took a trip to the third tier and back, with a couple more yo-yos after that for good measure, was seized upon by their neighbours United. The team, more recently described as 'noisy neighbours' by Sir Alex Ferguson, were similarly dismissed by United fans, who drew on local indie band Inspiral Carpets' hit 'This is How it Feels' to mock their rivals.

The song features the chorus 'This is how it feels to be lonely; this is how it feels to be small; this is how it feels when your life means nothing at all.'

It wasn't a great stretch for United to alter those lines, although there remains some debate whether it was them or their Greater Manchester neighbours Oldham who first used an alternative version of the song. Either way, here's United's version:

> This is how it feels to be City,
> This is how it feels to be small,
> This is how it feels when your team wins nothing at all

## ▦ STOKE NOT SHY

There's only ever been one Kajagoogoo-inspired football chant and, when it finally came, it was worth the wait. The obscure eighties new romantic outfit (below) hit the top of the charts with 'Too Shy', a song with a chorus that went 'Too shy-shy, hush, hush, ai-doo-aye'. Too young to remember? You didn't miss much.

Eighties footballers' poor pay packets led to some dubious style choices.

It was always going to take a unique set of circumstances for that chorus to inspire a football chant but when Stoke signed Turkish striker Tuncay Sanli in 2009, the missing piece of the jigsaw was found. Alongside his new teammates Robert Huth and Abdoulaye Faye, the Turk had unwittingly completed the quest for the most unlikey football chant of all time as the Stoke supporters sang:

Tun-cay, cay,
Huth, Huth, Abdoulaye!

## ▦ STENHOUSEMUIR FEATURE IN BOOK

What other book on British football culture would feature Stenhousemuir? The lowly Scottish club rarely receive mentions in dispatches north of the border, let alone further south, but they've made it here. That's because they were among the early adopters for using 'Love Will Tear Us Apart' as the inspiration for a chant, using it for midfielder Robert Love meaning they only had to change the 'us' to a 'you' and they were there.

Pretty soon, Man United were letting opponents know how Giggs would tear them apart and even cricket's Barmy Army celebrated Graeme Swann's bowling success against the Australians by singing that Swann would do likewise. But Aberdeen had been first with their ode to striker Steve Lovell, taking out the need even to sing the word 'will':

> Love,
> Lovell tear you apart, again

## ▦ EVERTON'S VANITY PROJECT

With their inflated salaries, flash cars and luxurious houses, today's Premier League footballers are often accused of greed and vanity. And that proved to be the basis for Everton's tribute to their England left-back Leighton Baines as the Goodison Park masses used Carly Simon's ironic chorus 'You're so vain, you probably think this song is about you' to great effect:

> Leighton Baines, you probably think this song is about you!

## ▦ HAPPY DAYS FOR THE GEORDIES

Newcastle fans have long been synonymous with passion due to the vociferous and heartfelt backing they always give their side. And that has led to some memorable numbers emerging from the Gallowgate end over the years. Faustino Asprilla, who used to celebrate his goals with trademark acrobatics across St James' Park, was the subject of one, to the tune of the 'Macarena':

There's only one Faustino Asprilla,
When he does a cartwheel you know he's scored a thriller,
He'll shit on United, the 'Pool and the Villa,
Tino Asprilla!

But perhaps the most inventive, and simultaneously amusing, effort of recent times from the Geordies is their ode to Habib Beye (pronounced Bay) as they used the former US TV sitcom *Happy Days*' theme tune and replaced the title with their hero's name. Simple, yet highly impressive:

Sunday, Monday, Habib Beye,
Tuesday, Wednesday, Habib Beye,
Thursday, Friday, Habib Beye,
Saturday, Habib Beye, rockin' all week with you!

# ▦ GINOLA SENDS TOON ARMY INTO LA LA LAND

Up there with Habib Beye's song, is the cracker that the Toon Army created for midfielder David Ginola. The skilful Frenchman had the fans eating out of the palm of his hands with his dazzling displays during a purple patch for the club which saw them come within touching distance of winning the Premier League.

The Toon Army used 'Lola' by The Kinks to sing the following (the main verses are included here, but there are others which some fans added):

He makes us sing and he makes us dance,
He's our superstar who comes from France,
It's Ginola – la la la Ginola
They say we've got the most fanatical fans,
And we've also got Les Ferdinand,
And Ginola – la la la Ginola

## THAT'S ZAMORA!

Brighton registered themselves in the football hit parade with their ode to free-scoring Bobby Zamora, based on Andy Williams' 'Amore':

> When the ball hits the goal
> It's not Shearer or Cole
> That's Zamora!

But, when Zamora was enduring a frustrating barren run after a fruitless spell at Spurs and an unsuccessful move to Fulham (at the time, he was later to hit form at Craven Cottage), the chant was soon rebooted to reflect his lack of goalscoring prowess:

> When you're sat in row Z
> And the ball hits your head
> That's Zamora!

## EVERYONE GIVES IT UP

Since Crystal Palace fans began chanting Jobi McAnuff's name to the KC and the Sunshine Band's seventies classic 'Give It Up', a chanting explosion has resulted with many teams adopting the tune.

The reason is simple. The only words to remember are the player's first name and surname and the rest of the song is made up of na, na, nas, mimicking the original hit. So whereas KC sung 'Na, na, na, na, na, na, na, na, na, na, na, baby give it up, give it up, baby give it up', Palace merely replaced the five syllables of baby give it up with Jobi McAnuff.

Pretty soon, teams across the land were desperately counting the syllables of their favourite players to see if they could adopt the chant. Spurs joined in with 'Rafael van der Vaart' (technically six syllables but why spoil a good song?) and rivals Arsenal got in on the act with Samir Nasri, despite this name clearly lacking the required syllabic mix. For the purposes of the chant, the Frenchman soon became 'Na-se-ri'.

The song has also been used by fans of teams showing promotion intent with Peterborough following the 'na-nas' with the five-syllable 'Posh are going up'. Expect this one to run and run.

# ▦ AUTOMATIC FOR THE CARDIFF PEOPLE

The Automatic's hit single 'Monster' spawned a full gig's worth of terrace chants but praise should go to Cardiff City for being quickest off the mark.

The Bluebirds are famous for original chants including 'The Ayatollah', which isn't actually a chant as it doesn't have any words and now features fans crouching down and making an 'ohhh' noise which builds to a crescendo, before they leap up and slap their own heads with both hands (it was started soon after the death of the Iranian spiritual leader Ayatollah Khomeini in 1989 as his followers repeatedly struck themselves as a customary sign of mourning).

With support like that, converting The Automatic's hit into a terrace chant was never going to be much of a problem and when City's Michael Chopra, on-loan from Newcastle, showed his eye for goal, there were his new fans waiting to salute him:

What's that coming over the hill?
It's Michael Chopra! It's Michael Chopra!

"Put your hands on your heads! Ha! Didn't say 'Simon Says'."

## ▦ CELTIC'S DISCO CLASSIC

When Celtic signed Italian striker Paolo Di Canio from AC Milan in 1996, it's fair to say that not many football fans in the UK knew who he was. But, by the time he'd also played for Sheffield Wednesday and West Ham – with an infamous shoving over of referee Paul Alcock along the way – there weren't many people who hadn't heard of the fiery Italian.

The Celtic fans knew that they had a cult hero on their hands and their song for him was truly inspired, their very own version of Ottawan's 'D.I.S.C.O':

> He is D, he's delightful,
> He is I, he's incredible,
> He is C, he's for Celtic,
> He is A, he's amazing,
> He is N, he's a natural,
> He is I, he's Italian,
> He is O, O, O!
> D I Canio! D I Canio!

## ▦ HESKEY'S WONDERLAND

The old Christmas hit 'Walking in a Winter Wonderland' has enjoyed something of a renaissance at football grounds across the country in recent times. It's usually used to herald a club hero with the lyrics staying true to the original, but beginning with 'There's Only One [insert name]' and then 'Walking along, singing a song, walking in a [insert name] wonderland.'

However, the better adaptations, have seen far more creativity, including Birmingham City's tribute to Emile Heskey. Despite his 62 England appearances and stacks of goals, the archetypal 'big front man' has always received a bad press and a hard time from fans. Blues supporters decided it was time to forgive and forget when he joined them from Liverpool in 2004:

> There's only one Emile Heskey,
> One Emile Heskey,
> He used to be shite,
> But now he's all right,
> Walking in a Heskey wonderland

# PALMER'S WONDERLAND

While Heskey's version wasn't overly flattering, it's unclear what Stockport manager Carlton Palmer would have made of his tribute by Hatters' fans.

Playing on a famous old chant which rhymed the midfielder's surname with marijuana, despite there having been no suggestion of Palmer ever having sampled the substance, Edgeley Park often rang out with the following inspired chant:

> There's only one Carlton Palmer
> And he smokes marijuana,
> He's six foot tall,
> His head's too small,
> Living in a Palmer wonderland!

# CADETE'S WONDERLAND

Naturally, 'Wonderland' has also been used to throw bile at opponents. Perhaps most infamously, certain fans target players and managers by singing their names for the first two lines, then chanting:

> With a packet of sweets
> And a cheeky smile
> [insert name] is a fucking paedophile

But, Rangers fans managed to be insulting – and fairly amusing – at the same time with their song for Celtic's prolific Portuguese striker Jorge Cadete [pronounced Ca-detee]. In the mid-nineties, Parkhead was wowed by Cadete's goalscoring and equally by his wild, flowing locks, which would bounce on his shoulders as he wheeled away in delight every time he scored. Rangers fans were having none of it, though, as they sung:

> There's only one Jorge Cadete,
> He's got hair like spaghetti,
> He's Portuguese,
> He's one of these, [make universal male masturbation hand gesture]
> Walking in a Laudrup wonderland

## ▥ WIFE SWAP

Staying with the classics, Frankie Valli's 'Can't Take My Eyes Off You' has also made itself heard around the grounds over the last decade. Arsenal's ode to one-time dyed-red-haired Swedish forward Freddie Ljungberg was probably the first time the tune had been used as they chanted:

> We love you Freddie
> Because you've got red hair,
> We love you Freddie
> Because you're everywhere,
> We love you Freddie,
> You're Arsenal through and through

Other copies came and went, but it was West Ham fans who laid down a new marker – which went on to be sung for fans' heroes at many other grounds – with this tribute to Scottish defender Christian Dailly:

> Oh Christian Dailly,
> You are the love of my life,
> Oh Christian Dailly,
> I'd let you shag my wife,
> Oh Christian Dailly,
> You've got curly hair too!

## ▥ THE YOUTH TEAM

Of all the hit singles in this chapter, without any doubt the most unlikely to become the basis for a terrace chant would have to be Musical Youth's 'Pass the Dutchie'.

Although whether this one actually became a major chant is highly unlikely given the sketchy information that's known about it. However, it is believed that some (probably not that many) West Ham fans used to sing the famous chorus to the Musical Youth song to serenade their left-back, along these lines:

> Paul Konchesky on de left-hand side!

# LARSSON TURNS BRUMMIE HEADS

And on the subject of unlikely conversions from the charts to the terraces, Kylie Minogue's 'Can't Get You Out of My Head' is also up there. Birmingham City winger Sebastian Larsson was the subject of this particular reimagined masterpiece with its catchy opening 'la la' sequence making it especially football-fan friendly:

> La, la, la, la, la, la-Larsson
> La, la, la, la, la, la-Larsson
> We just can't get enough of our Seb,
> He is all us Brummies think about

# REBEL WITHOUT A CAUSE

It takes a special type of player to have more than one song chanted for him and Gary Neville is that sort of player. Idolised by Manchester United fans because of his unashamedly anti-Liverpool views, he's the player who fans know would be standing alongside them if he wasn't actually on the pitch. In fact, upon announcing his retirement in early 2011, Neville did exactly that, taking his seat behind the goal for United's away fixture against Chelsea.

Apart from his 'Gary Neville is a Red' signature tune, United fans also sang a David Bowie number to hail their trusty right-back. 'Rebel Rebel' was the tune they chose, and they just about got away with it too:

(It's also worth noting that Neville's father has the first name Neville too, to help enjoyment of this chant even more.)

> Neville Neville, you play in defence,
> Neville Neville, your play is immense,
> Neville Neville, like Jacko you're bad,
> Neville Neville is the name of your dad!

# KING KETSBAIA

Singing chart songs for terrace tunes is certainly not just a British thing. The use of 'Seven Nation Army' began in Europe, and fans of Greek club Olympiakos took the genre to a whole new level with their chant for new manager Temuri Ketsbaia (pronounced Kets-buyer). The Georgian, a former Newcastle, Wolves and Dundee player, was serenaded to the tune of Kings of Leon's 'Sex on Fire' with the simple lyrics:

Woah-oh-woah
Temuri Ketsbaia!

## ▦ STEVENAGE CAN'T HELP THEMSELVES

Stevenage may be relative newcomers to the Football League but that hasn't stopped them expressing themselves on the terraces. In fact, bringing with them the originality and freedom of the non-League football scene may possibly give their fans an advantage over the jaded and cynical long-suffering lower division supporters.

Used to success for several years, when their team are winning Stevenage fans belt out the following, to the tune of 'I Can't Help Falling in Love With You':

You are shit,
And you always were,
And we can't help scoring more goals than you!

# TONY CASCARINO

**If ever there was an archetypal 'big striker' it was Tony Cascarino.**
The 6ft 3in target man was devastating in the air and scored more than
250 goals for the likes of Chelsea, Marseille and the Republic of Ireland.
As a result of these feats, he built up a fine array of chants with which fans
used to worship him, one of which he still holds dearest.

'At Marseille they used to sing "Tonygoal" [to the
tune of "Here We Go"] which they probably wouldn't
have sung anywhere else. When I was playing for
Ireland, they sang "Tony Cascarino" [to tune of "What
a load of rubbish" but clearly not referencing that point]
while at Millwall, it was "There's only one Cascarino" but
they used that for everyone.

'At Villa, it was "We've got Tony, Cascarino, we've got
Tony in the air "[to the tune of "Ging Gang Goolie"].
But my favourite one has to be at Chelsea. It started
in the dressing room. Bob Ward, who was the
physio at the time, started singing it to a Tina
Turner song, and I told one of my mates. Wisey
[Dennis] would take the piss a bit when Bob sang
it, as there was a lot of banter flying about the
dressing room. We played at White Hart Lane and
my mate got into the Chelsea end. I wasn't that
popular at the time, but I scored a hat-trick, and he
started singing it on his own – other fans joined in
and it went from there:

> We don't need another hero,
> We've got Tony Cascarino!

Cas liked to keep his spare toilet rolls on him at all times.

# TOPICAL
# CHANTS

Certain situations lend themselves to comedy and that's why many stand-up artists will focus on relationships or sex. In the same way, there are certain events that may have taken place around a football match, that lend themselves to more spontaneous chants from the quicker-witted fans. This chapter is a celebration of those moments of genius and a doffing of the hat to the fans who saw the funny side of what weren't always the most comedic scenarios.

## ANDY-CAPPED

When it was revealed in the press that Rangers and Scotland goalkeeper Andy Goram had been diagnosed as suffering from mild schizophrenia, there was no way his own fans would make light of that, right? Wrong. With perhaps the cruellest-yet-funniest chant of all time, the Ibrox faithful used the usual 'Guantanamera' tribute song to salute their man, with a slight twist:

*Two Andy Gorams,*
*There's only two Andy Gorams!*

## COLCHESTER'S YULETIDE FOG

It's a longstanding tradition for fans of a team that's winning to taunt their opponents as much as possible. Thus, towards the end of a game when one side is in the ascendancy, their fans will often mock opposition supporters as they head for the exits. At Colchester's Weston Homes Community Stadium, the home team were 2-0 up against Southampton in a 2009 Christmas fixture when freezing fog descended over the stadium in the closing stages of the match. Latching onto this bizarre situation, where it was barely possible to see from one end of the ground to the other, the home fans began chanting to the Saints' contingent (to the tune of 'Bread of Heaven'):

*We can't see you sneaking out!*

## POMPEY PAY THE PRICE

Another floodlight failure was greeted by a different chant altogether when Portsmouth played Leeds at Fratton Park in early 2011. The lights went out twice during the second half and, after hearing the Pompey fans singing their usual anthem of 'Play up Pompey' (to the tune of 'Westminster Chimes') throughout the game, the Leeds fans sung their own version in the darkness at the cash-strapped club:

*Pay up Pompey,*
*Pompey pay up!*

## ▦ EDMUNDO'S MONKEY BUSINESS

Some chants have passed into football folklore without any confirmation of whether they were actually sung. This being a book which has been meticulously researched and fact-checked, none of those were able to be included. Except this one.

Legend has it that in 1999 Brazilian striker Edmundo hired a circus to perform in his garden to mark his son's birthday. Legend also has it that the visiting chimpanzee Pedrinho was allegedly plied with beer and whiskey by the footballer until it was quite drunk. And legend really has it that when news of this alleged incident reached the UK, some football fans composed the following chant to 'Quartermaster's Store':

> He shot,
> He missed,
> He got a monkey pissed,
> Edmundo, Edmundo!

## ▦ ROONEY'S TEARS OF SHAME

With the advent of the super-injunction, the days of footballers' extra-curricular activities being exposed in the tabloid press may become a thing of the past. Which would be a terrible shame for the rich crop of football chants that stem from such scandal.

When Wayne Rooney was reported to have allegedly paid prostitute Jennifer Thompson for sex several times over a six-month period while his wife was pregnant with their future son Kai, the knives were out for the Manchester United and England star. Everton, Rooney's former club, were due to face United in a league match soon after and the fans had the following chant prepared for their former hero to the tune of the Bob Marley classic:

> No woman, no Kai

Unfortunately for them, Sir Alex Ferguson thought it wise to rest Rooney from the game, meaning he never heard the inspired ditty.

## ▦ GIGGS'S BEANS ARE SPILLED

Continuing on the super-injunction theme, 22 May 2011 should have been a day of celebration for Manchester United's Ryan Giggs. About to be presented with an unprecedented 12th Premier League winners' medal as United capped off another title-winning season, Giggs was supposed to be surveying the scene with satisfaction.

But a series of lurid tabloid revelations about his private life, which he'd tried to prevent from publication, had finally been printed and the visiting Blackpool fans had a subtle song to remind him of his actions. Despite their impending relegation, the Tangerine Army sang (to 'Bread of Heaven'):

> You're not secret,
> You're not secret,
> You're not secret anymore!

A super-injunction prevents us from publishing this caption.

## BRIEFS ENCOUNTER

It's hard to believe that many football chants have been composed based on an exchange in a courtroom, but Leeds United conjured up a classic for Lee Bowyer. During a trial in which the midfielder was accused of an assault on Sarfraz Najeib in Leeds city centre during a night out, the footballer was asked by his QC to change into the trousers and shoes he had been wearing on that night.

The subsequent exchange led to the revelation that Bowyer had, in fact, turned up for court 'commando' style – without pants. Sure enough, eagle-eyed Leeds fans who were following the trial had a moment of inspiration at the next United game as they sang the classic football tribute song to all-action midfielders who cover every blade of grass, although with one subtle change:

> He's here,
> He's there,
> He wears no underwear,
> Lee Bowyer, Lee Bowyer!

## TOTTENHAM'S KITCHEN NIGHTMARES

It may not have been an epic battle to land the league title, but the scene was set for an incredible last-day showdown between arch-rivals Tottenham and Arsenal in 2006. Up for grabs was fourth place and a coveted spot in the following season's Champions League. A win for Tottenham would have guaranteed them that fourth spot with Arsenal waiting in the wings, should their neighbours slip up.

Incredibly, six Tottenham players were taken ill with suspected food poisoning in the early hours of match day – all had eaten lasagne at the buffet at the team hotel the night before. Police were even called as foul play was suspected but nothing was proved and Spurs were forced to field a team containing players who were clearly drained of sleep and energy. They lost 2-1 while Arsenal beat Wigan 4-2 and the Champions League dream was over for Martin Jol's team.

Scarcely believing their luck at the chanting material on offer, the Arsenal fans put their own 'Volare' tune to good use:

Lasagne, woah-oh,
Lasagne, woah-oh,
We laughed ourselves to bits,
When Tottenham got the shits!

## WHEN IN ZURICH ...

European competitions tend to lend themselves to more imaginative chants as British fans find themselves in new environments with new stereotypes to toy with.

With a UEFA Cup match in Switzerland against FC Zurich, Newcastle United fans would have had plenty of time on their journey to plan something special – and they didn't disappoint. When Silvio Maric broke the deadlock early in the second half, the Geordie fans immediately burst into song to taunt their hosts:

You're not yodelling,
You're not yodelling,
You're not yodelling any more!

## CHELSEA'S TURKISH DELIGHT

And in a similar vein, the expansion of the Champions League into its current format has meant that English clubs are taking on foreign opposition with greater regularity than ever before. And with those matches comes the opportunity to experiment.

Chelsea welcomed Galatasaray to London for a Champions League match in 1999 and the Stamford Bridge crowd adapted a version of a traditional English song specially for their Turkish guests (to the tune of 'Go West'):

You're shish,
And you know you are!

## ☷ LEFT OUT IN THE COLE

As has already been noted, football fans have no mercy when it comes to riling the opposition – or their players – for any reason.

Already a deeply unpopular player due to his infamously petulant disregard for Arsenal's offer to pay him 'only' £55,000 per week, Ashley Cole has long been a target for abuse by the so-called boo boys. He even got it in the neck from England fans during an international against Kazakhstan at Wembley when a sloppy back pass allowed the visitors to score – so he was hardly going to get off lightly following the breakdown of his marriage to pop star Cheryl Cole.

Her hit single 'Fight For This Love' which contained the chorus 'We gotta fight, fight, fight, fight, fight for this love' was bastardised by Stoke fans to taunt the left-back at Stamford Bridge when it appeared that the couple were going to separate for good:

You gotta file, file, file, file, file for divorce!

## ☷ SCOTLAND PLAY WITH THEMSELVES

Scotland's loyal Tartan Army follow their team all over the globe and have become accustomed to almost anything, especially given their country's less than impressive recent record. However, nothing could have prepared those fans for the events in Tallinn, Estonia, on 9 October 1996.

The night before, the Scots' manager Craig Brown had raised concerns about the quality of the floodlights that were due to be used for the 6.45pm kick off and the visitors had their complaint upheld by FIFA, who ordered the World Cup qualifier to be played at 3pm. The arrangement was not to the liking of the Estonians who refused to turn up at the new start time.

Incredibly, just before 3pm the Scottish team walked out onto the pitch alone, along with the referee and two linesmen – who actually checked the goal nets as if a meaningful match was about to be played. The Scots lined up in their usual formation, despite having no opponents in the other half of the pitch, and when the referee blew his whistle, Billy Dodds rolled the ball forward to John Collins only for the referee to blow his whistle and immediately call a halt to proceedings.

And this entire fiasco took place in front of 1,000 travelling Scottish fans, who ironically chanted 'get in tae them' before the start of the 'match' but saved their best for last as they chanted to 'Guantanamera':

One team in Tallinn,
There's only one team in Tallinn!

## ▦ REF COMES UP SHORT

All away fans watching their team in the ascendancy will enjoy rubbing it in the locals' faces by chanting 'You're supposed to be at home' to the tune of 'Bread of Heaven'. But fans at a Port Vale v Lincoln game sang an updated version of this song when they discovered their referee for the day was below average height. Just for a moment, the official became the centre of attention as fans chanted:

You're supposed to be a gnome!

## ▦ POLL'S FINAL STRAW

Another official who inadvertently became the centre of attention was Graham Poll. One of England's top-rated referees, Poll was often asked to perform on the highest stage. Unfortunately for him, sometimes the biggest occasion proved too much as infamously illustrated by his cock-up during a World Cup match between Croatia and Australia in 2006.

During the game, the English official managed to book Croatian Josip Simunic on three separate occasions, finally flourishing a red card only after the third yellow. Not ideal in a Sunday morning game, and utterly humiliating in a match taking place on the global stage. The *Sun* highlighted the incident with the headline 'Three Card Thick'.

'OK, that's his second red. One more and he's off.'

Sadly for Poll, back in England, the fans offered him little sympathy and at a Carling Cup match at Goodison Park a few months later, Everton and Arsenal fans united in singing the following to 'Go West':

> World Cup
> And you fucked it up!

## TERRY'S BRIDGE OF SIGHS

After reports of John Terry's alleged affair with the ex-girlfriend of team-mate Wayne Bridge had appeared in the press, opposition fans revelled in his misfortune and dozens of chants could be heard across the country consisting of varying levels of cruelty. One of the best was created by Manchester United fans, who also managed to work in a dig at bitter rivals Liverpool for good measure. This was sung to the 'Lord of the Dance' tune:

> Chelsea, wherever you may be,
> Don't leave your wife with John Terry.
> It could be worse, he could be Scouse,
> He'd fuck your wife,
> Then he'd rob your house!

## TERRY'S OWN COLE

Even Wolves fans managed to get in on the act when the two clubs met. Their take was much more simplistic – if you're going to have it away with someone close to one of your teammates, make it worthwhile. This one goes to the tune of 'Guantanamera':

> Shagged Cheryl Cole,
> You should've shagged Cheryl Cole!

# ▦ NO BELL PEACE PRIZE

It is a universally acknowledged truth that whenever Portsmouth take to the field, one of their fans will ring a bell from the stands throughout the match. That fan is none other than Mr John Anthony Portsmouth Football Club Westwood and he is probably his club's – if not English football's – most recognisable supporter. Quite what the Pompey fans who sit within earshot of the incessant bell ringing make of him is unclear, but there is no Portsmouth without his Pompey Chimes – apart from during one game at Highbury.

During this particular encounter, Pompey were being taken to the cleaners by the Gunners despite the bell. Towards the end of the game, for reasons that remain unclear, Westwood – and his bell – were asked to leave. And, by way of celebration, the Arsenal fans deftly altered the words of an everyday chant to sing:

> You're not ringing anymore!

# ▦ SHEARER'S HOBSON'S CHOICE

Imagine the dilemma. You have a cushy job with easy hours and few worries when the love of your life comes calling, asking you to save them from a serious predicament. No man can stick their head in the sand in those circumstances. Although Alan Shearer probably wishes he had.

The former Newcastle United striker was settling nicely into BBC sofas in his role as a *Match of the Day* pundit when the SOS call came from St James' Park. Shearer had eight games to save his beloved club from relegation. In what was always going to be a tough ask, he was destined to fail, winning only once in his short spell. And during a 3-0 defeat at Liverpool, the ever-witty Kop serenaded the temporary gaffer with this chant to 'Guantanamera':

> Stayed on the telly,
> You should've stayed on the telly!

## ▦ VILLA STAR'S NEW STRIP

The days of footballers preparing for a big match by getting as drunk as possible the night before are long gone. But, sometimes the antics of previous generations of players are repeated by their more 'professional' descendants.

When Aston Villa's John Carew was spotted by fans at a Birmingham lap-dancing club the night before his team's UEFA Cup tie against Ajax, he was always going to have trouble explaining himself. He was subsequently fined by manager Martin O'Neill, although the player told the *Birmingham Post*: 'I wasn't at the strip club but the bar which shares the same entrance. The whole thing is a misunderstanding.'

That story wasn't bought by Villa fans either and at the following home game, a 4-0 stroll over Wigan in which the Norwegian came off the bench to score, they sang this to the tune of 'Que Sera, Sera':

> John Carew, Carew,
> He likes a lap-dance or two,
> He might even pay for you,
> John Carew, Carew

## ▦ CITY SWINGERS

When famed lothario and occasional football manager Sven-Göran Eriksson took over at Manchester City, he was never going to hit the headlines for the action on the pitch. Although City did relatively well under the Swede, it was his action elsewhere that made the front pages as a series of flings were exposed by the press. And the club's impressed fans were quick off the mark with a celebratory tribute song, to the tune of 'Lord of the Dance':

> Sven, Sven, wherever you may be,
> You are the pride of Man City,
> You can shag my wife on our settee,
> If we get to Wem-ber-lee!

Fortunately for all concerned, City were knocked out of the FA Cup in round four that season.

## ░ INDECENT PROPOSAL

With the huge popularity of football going into overdrive in the last two decades, fans have had increased opportunity to show their loyalty to their clubs. From having their ashes scattered on the pitch to taking wedding vows in the centre circle, anything is now possible.

And when a Hull City fan decided to go onto the KC Stadium pitch at half-time of a 2008 Championship match against West Brom to propose to his girlfriend, he probably thought he was onto a winner. But he hadn't banked on the away fans spoiling his moment as the Baggies used a chant usually reserved for referees:

They went on to spend their honeymoon at the club's training ground.

*You don't know what you're doing!*

## ░ GARY GETS THE BLUES

Birmingham City striker Gary O'Connor celebrated the start of his newly promoted side's 2007/08 Premier League campaign in spectacular style. The *News of the World* reported that O'Connor and his friends allegedly hosted four prostitutes in a plush hotel room on the eve of the new season.

In an unconnected event, the £2.7 million striker subsequently found himself on the bench with manager Alex McLeish informing him his 'fitness' had to improve to warrant a first team place. Obviously. Blues' fans wasted little time by composing this chant to the tune of 'Volare' for their reserve forward:

*Gary O'Connor, woah-oh,*
*Gary O'Connor, woah-oh,*
*He shagged a prostitute,*
*Now he's a substitute!*

## NEWCASTLE SWEAR BY KINNEAR

Newcastle United's rollercoaster relegation season of 2008/09 featured four different managers (the last one being Alan Shearer as mentioned above). But the most unforgettable was Joe Kinnear. The old-school, no-nonsense gaffer was convinced the media were being unnecessarily hostile towards him. And during one extraordinary press conference just a week into his tenure, Kinnear lost the plot with *Daily Mirror* reporter Simon Bird. The Toon Army conjured up an instant classic chant to the tune of 'Quartermaster's Store':

He's fat, he's round,
He swears like Chubby Brown,
Joe Kinnear, Joe Kinnear!

'I say old chap! Could that possibly have been offside?'

## ▤ HAMMERS HUMOUR

The funniest football chants usually emerge from fans who are not afraid to laugh at themselves – unfortunately, some of them don't have much of a choice.

When West Ham supporters were staring relegation in the face in their penultimate match of the 2010/11 Premier League season away to Wigan, they would've been surprised to see their team go 2-0 up, therefore placing the Latics in a perilous position themselves. Sensing a unique opportunity to make light of the double jeopardy facing both teams on the pitch, the Hammers fans began chanting to the tune of 'Guantanamera':

> Down with the West Ham,
> You're going down with the West Ham!

The fun in the away end did not stop there as the visiting fans also used the traditional chant sung by teams celebrating an impending Wembley appearance, to make light of their imminent demotion.

> Que sera, sera,
> Whatever will be will be,
> We're going to Coventry,
> Que sera, sera

## ▤ EVERTON BOSS YOSS

Sport and politics have never mixed well but some football fans will stop at nothing to put off an opposition player.

When Everton faced a Liverpool side featuring Israeli international Yossi Benayoun, the Toffees couldn't resist a political dig at the midfielder. Using the Beach Boys' 'Sloop John B', they offered one of the more bizarre topical chants ever heard in a British stadium:

> The Gaza's not yours,
> The Gaza's not yours,
> Yossi Benayoun,
> The Gaza's not yours

# STAN COLLYMORE

**A playing career that took him everywhere from Nottingham Forest to Liverpool saw Stan Collymore realise many boyhood dreams.** But none compared to playing for his hometown club Aston Villa. And it's a Villa chant which Collymore has picked for his favourite, one that is unique to the club as Villa fans have been singing 'Holte Enders in the Sky' since the sixties. It's sung to the tune of Johnny Cash's 'Ghost Riders in the Sky'.

'I first went to Villa in 1977 for a 0-0 draw against Derby and I fell asleep at half time,' says Collymore. 'My heroes growing up were Gary Shaw and Peter Withe, who led us to title and European Cup victories in 1981 and 1982 respectively. But my proudest moment in a Villa shirt was scoring a hat-trick in Europe, which only Shaw, Withe and I have managed! 'My favourite chant is: "Yippee-aye-ay, Yippee-aye-oh, Holte Enders in the sky". I've sung it loudly and proudly since the early eighties and it's unique to the Villa.'

Stan the Man couldn't believe his luck when the Arsenal defender started breakdancing.

# 4

# TERRACE
# BANTER

There are many occasions when opposing fans exchange chants with each other, with off-the-cuff responses in defence of their club or at the expense of the opposing team. And it's these exchanges which still provide the great humour and improvisation for which British football fan culture is so famed. This chapter celebrates those moments when the game of football being played almost becomes secondary, and the banter, passion and honour between rival fans takes centre stage.

## ▦ OOHING AND AHHING

It's hard to think of many non-English chants that have been heard at a British football ground, but Leeds fans surpassed themselves back in 1995. When Eric Cantona was enduring a long spell on the sidelines following his infamous kung-fu kick on a Crystal Palace fan, Man United took on Leeds and continued to sing their Cantona tribute 'Ooh-ahh Cantona' usually chanted to the tune of the French national anthem 'La Marseillaise' (or occasionally to 'Go West'). Sensing a unique opportunity, Leeds fans countered with:

> Ou est Eric Cantona?

## ▦ CHAMPIONS LEAGUE? YOU'RE HAVING A LAUGH

The dry wit and self-deprecation of Liverpool fans has earned them a reputation as one of the country's funniest set of supporters, but even they were stumped by relative minnows Wigan Athletic.

The Scousers are famous for celebrating the fact they're the most successful English team in the European Cup with five wins, regularly chanting to the tune of 'Sloop John B':

> We've won it five times,
> We've won it five times,
> In Istanbul
> We won it five times

For a long time after their 2005 triumph over AC Milan in Turkey, Liverpool fans would sing this home and away but on one trip to Wigan, they were met by a rival chant with a level of self-deprecation that blew the wind right out of their sails.

The Latics have no history to match the Anfield club, and their shock rise to the English top flight was aided by owner Dave Whelan's healthy bank balance. However, on their way they did pick up a number of trophies, hence the following retort from Wigan's regulars:

We've won it two times
We've won it two times
Auto Windscreens
We've won it two times!

(Stoke City, themselves two-time winners of the Football League Trophy of which Wigan so proudly sing, also use this chant against Liverpool but an independent panel of adjudicators has found that Wigan were first.)

## ▦ LIVERPOOL SING IN STEREO

That was a rare example of the Liverpool fans being rendered silent by an opposition chant – a few years earlier in a match against West Ham, the Anfield club's loyal followers showed they have no qualms about laughing at themselves.

One of the most common subjects for chants aimed at Liverpool references the city's crime and unemployment problems – fans usually sing about car theft or encouraging the Liverpool fans to 'sign on' and 'get a job'. The Anfield fans have clearly become accustomed to this and are more than happy to use the stereotype as a pre-emptive way to silence opposition fans.

In February 2001, the Reds were hosting the Hammers, who boasted Italian striker Paolo Di Canio among their ranks. The visiting fans were singing 'We've got Di Canio' to the usual Italian operatic tones, but the home fans countered with their own version:

You've got Di Canio,
We've got your stereo!

(According to Liverpool fan and author Peter Etherington, this chant was first sung at a pub after the game between the clubs in London earlier that season, then aired again at the return match.)

## ▦ UNITED'S ARSENAL HERO

Although not geographical rivals, Arsenal and Manchester United fans have come to loathe each other over the years, be it for North v South pride or, more recently, due to the clubs fighting for the game's major honours.

The 1998/99 season boiled down to a battle between the two teams for both the FA Cup and the Premier League, with Arsenal defending the Double they'd won the previous season driven on by their midfield powerhouse Patrick Vieira. Gunners' fans always saluted Vieira with his song to the tune of 'Volare':

> Vieira, woah-oh,
> Vieira, woah-oh,
> He came from Se-ne-gal
> To play for Ar-se-nal!

The clubs met in the FA Cup semi-final, which went to a replay that many observers regard as one of the finest games of football ever played in England. Although the league title was still to be decided, it was clear that whoever prevailed in this titanic clash would have the psychological edge for the remaining league fixtures.

Just when penalties seemed likely, Arsenal hero Vieira misplaced a pass straight into the path of United's Ryan Giggs, who proceeded to run half the length of the pitch and famously score the winning goal. The United fans went on to celebrate an historic Treble while Arsenal were left empty-handed – and silenced by the United song which emerged soon after:

> Vieira, woah-oh,
> Vieira, woah-oh,
> He gave Giggsy the ball
> And Arsenal won fuck all!

## THE HISTORY BOYS

There has been little love lost between Chelsea and Liverpool fans in recent years. Since Roman Abramovich's millions signalled a transformation in the west London club's fortunes, the two teams found themselves sharing top billing in the Premier League and the Champions League.

Liverpool's fans, as is their way, prepared for these clashes with their own song which reminded their London rivals of their proud record (to the tune of 'Lord of the Dance'):

Fuck off, Chelsea FC,
You ain't got no history.
Five European Cups and 18 leagues,
That's what we call history

This chant was sung with gusto by the Kop whenever Chelsea visited (and when their own regulars made the trip down to Stamford Bridge) but on 2 May 2010, the tables were turned as the Kop's chant was rammed back down their throats. The Blues had been battling Manchester United to win the Premier League with all Liverpool fans knowing that a United victory would have meant a 19th title, eclipsing their own longstanding record.

And as Frank Lampard put Chelsea 2-0 up at Anfield to all but secure the title and end United's hopes, the away fans made the following point to their hosts with this chant to their favourite operatic tune 'La Donna è Mobile':

We saved your history,
We saved your history!

## ▦ PLUMBING THE DEPTHS

At the other end of football's glamour scale, there was an amusing exchange between Sheffield Wednesday and Crystal Palace fans at the end of the same season. The Championship clubs were involved in a relegation battle to the death as they met at Hillsborough on the last day of the season with the losers heading down to League One.

A seesaw encounter ended with Palace, who were in severe financial trouble at the time and had been docked 10 points for going into administration, staying up on account of a 2-2 draw. The Eagles fans mocked the dejected Wednesday faithful by chanting 'Going down, going down, going down!' (to the tune of 'Here We Go' or, as it's better known, 'Stars and Stripes Forever') at them. But, at their lowest ebb, the home fans still had the sense of humour to respond to their visitors by singing: 'Going bust, going bust, going bust!'

## ▦ SING WHEN YOU'RE WINNING

When Celtic were being taught a footballing lesson by Arsenal in a 2009 Champions League qualifier, their fans had the good sense to at least mock the silent home masses – or so they thought. Playing on the traditional stereotype of Arsenal's indifferent home fans, the Glaswegians, at least 4-0 behind on aggregate at the time, chanted the familiar:

*Shall we sing a song for you?*

But, the quiet Emirates Stadium support soon found its voice as it volleyed straight back with:

*Shall we score a goal for you?*

## ▦ STOKE RUGGER BUGGERS

Arsenal were on the wrong end of some quick-witted chanting a couple of seasons later at the hands of Stoke City. Some unlikely animosity had sprung up between the clubs as a result of a poor challenge by Stoke's Ryan

Kenwyne Jones's blow football skills had come up trumps again.

Shawcross on Arsenal's Aaron Ramsey, who suffered a double leg fracture and a lengthy recuperation spell.

Arsenal manager Arsène Wenger was convinced the foul had been deliberate and went out of his way to tell anyone who would listen. And following a game between Stoke and Tottenham in 2010, Wenger spoke out about a Shawcross challenge on the Spurs goalkeeper Heurelho Gomes despite the fact his team weren't involved in the match: 'You cannot say it is football any more,' he said. 'It is more rugby on the goalkeepers than football.' Shawcross countered by saying: 'He's obviously got something against me. It's just weird. He seems to have a problem with Stoke, our manager and certain players.'

The chain of events meant the league match between the clubs at the Britannia Stadium, where incidentally the home fans have been recorded as being the loudest in the country, would be keenly contested to say the least. But, in fact, Arsenal didn't offer much of a fight and Stoke were two goals up before half-time. Their fans, who hadn't forgotten Wenger's comments, used 'Go West' to chant:

2-0 to the rugby team!

And if that hadn't rubbed it in enough, towards the end of Stoke's 3-1 win, most home fans were singing the Twickenham anthem 'Swing Low, Sweet Chariot'.

## REDS' BLUES

And on the subject of not winning trophies, Man United fans have always taken great pleasure in turning around their great rivals' chant to suit themselves.

Liverpool have spent several years travelling around the country with a familiar chant of 'Li-ver-pool, Li-ver-pool' ringing around every ground, each syllable being emphasised. But, United fans were quick to make sure their rivals wouldn't risk singing that again whenever the two teams met by quickly changing the three syllables as follows:

Li-ver-pool, win fuck all

# ▓ ARSENAL CAN'T BEAR TEDDY

When a spur-of-the-moment chant is called for, sometimes lyrical wit and subtle nuances have to be sacrificed in the name of making a point.

Teddy Sheringham had always proved to be something of a thorn in the side of Arsenal fans. As a Tottenham striker in the nineties, he was never going to be popular at Highbury, but his departure to Man United in 1997 meant he was even more of a target for abuse by Gooners as the two clubs were competing for major silverware.

The move to Old Trafford was widely seen as Sheringham's attempt to land the honours that were missing from his otherwise exemplary CV but, when Arsenal won the Double in 1998, the striker was left empty-handed again to the delight of the Highbury masses, who sang (to the tune of 'Son of My Father'):

> Oh Teddy, Teddy,
> He went to Man United and he won fuck all

However, the following season, Sheringham was to finally earn the trophies he craved – and in spectacular style too as United landed a unique Treble of FA Cup, Premier League and Champions League.

When United took on Arsenal the season after the Treble, their fans were keen to sing their own version of the song with which their striker had been taunted:

> Oh Teddy Teddy,
> He went to Man United and he won the lot!

But, the Highbury hatred of Sheringham knew no bounds and, almost immediately, the Arsenal fans replied:

> Oh Teddy Teddy,
> He went to Man United and he's still a c*nt

# JASON CUNDY

**Jason Cundy may not have enjoyed the most glittering football career, especially as injuries forced him to retire from the game early.** But the former defender certainly made his mark on a different side of the game when he hit the headlines after being diagnosed with testicular cancer in 1997. At that time, the male-specific version of the illness was still a taboo subject, but thanks to Cundy's recovery and his subsequent work with the Everyman charity, he played a part in helping to change male awareness of the problem. And ironically, it's Cundy's illness that provides him with his selected terrace tune, although for all the wrong reasons.

'Even though I wouldn't say this is my favourite as such,' says Cundy, 'this was a chant that was sung at me and I was happy to laugh it off. It was while I was playing for Ipswich, and shortly after my recovery from testicular cancer. I think I went to take a throw in and the fans started singing: "One ball, he's only got one ball" [to the tune of "Blue Moon"]. I did have a laugh about it. I thought that was the best way to handle it!'

It was an extreme reaction to winning a corner.

# THE CHANTS
# THAT SHOCKED
# FOOTBALL

Football fans have few qualms about unleashing their take on the personal tragedies that may have befallen their rivals. This is *not* the chapter for people who are easily offended; it's the chapter Frankie Boyle might have written, if he was actually a football fan and not busy thinking of jokes about Katie Price's kid. So we move onwards and, er, downwards to some of the most depraved, offensive and vindictive chants that have ever been sung in British football grounds.

# ▦ POSH CAN TAKE IT

David Beckham has been subjected to many appalling chants during his career as fans rounded on his success and popularity. Mrs Beckham – or Posh Spice as the tabloids christened her – was also an obvious target and, once their impending nuptials were announced, it wasn't long before Leeds fans and many other United rivals were using this song to the tune of 'Go West':

> Posh Spice, takes it up the arse,
> Posh Spice, takes it up the arse!

The chant was heard so often at United games that it was impossible for either Mr or Mrs Beckham to ignore it – instead, they did the clever thing and laughed at it as this memorable exchange from a Comic Relief interview they undertook with the Sacha Baron Cohen character Ali G shows:

Ali G: Now there's a really insulting song that they sing about you. Have you heard it? What is the words?

Victoria: I can't repeat that really, it's pretty insulting.

Ali G: But have you heard it?

Beckham: No I haven't heard it.

Victoria: Well, what is it?

Ali G: Well I heard something, is it about you... taking... it... up... ?

Victoria: Oh yeah, yeah, OK... It's Posh Spice... (mouths 'takes it up the arse').

Ali G: So you take it up the arse!

Victoria: No!

Ali G: That ain't an insult, that is the biggest compliment you can get!

Victoria: You're just saying that 'cos you're a bit of a batty boy yourself.

Ali G: You is crossing dangerous territory! All I can say is that I wish they would sing that about me Julie. Nah but serious, do you take it up the arse?

Victoria: Of course I don't.

Ali G: (to Beckham) So you telling me you ain't never been caught offside?

Beckham: No!

Ali G always dressed his best for the dentist.

## ▦ POSH TAKES IT AGAIN

Not satisfied with the crudeness of the original song, Leeds fans came up with a new ditty which had the combined effect of insulting Beckham and saluting one of their own heroes at the same time.

Leeds had already come up with the innovative 'Harry, Harry Kewell' to the tune of Boney M classic 'Daddy Cool' but they paid their winger the ultimate compliment with this chant to the tune of 'My Old Man's a Dustman':

> Posh Spice is a slapper,
> She wears a big fat jewel,
> And when she's shagging Beckham,
> She thinks of Harry Kewell!

There were a number of variations on this particular chant as other rival fans would insert the name of their own heroes instead of Kewell. Tottenham fans created a particularly amusing version:

> Posh Spice is a slapper,
> She wears a Wonderbra,
> And when she's shagging Beckham,
> She thinks of Ginola!

## ▦ SHIELDS UNPROTECTED IN MANCHESTER

When Liverpool fan Michael Shields was celebrating his side's extraordinary 2005 Champions League win in Bulgaria with friends, he could never have envisaged the dramatic way his life was about to change.

Shields was involved in a drunken fracas in which a Bulgarian man received severe head injuries and the Liverpudlian was subsequently charged with attempted murder and jailed for 15 years, which was reduced to ten on appeal. Shields was eventually transferred to a British prison and, after a campaign protesting his innocence, he received a Royal pardon and was released in 2009.

Given that the city of Liverpool was outraged by Shields' original predicament, it was entirely predictable that Man United fans would make the most of their rivals' misfortune and come up with this song to the tune of Johnny Cash's 'Ring of Fire' which itself had become an Anfield favourite:

Michael Shields got ten more years,
In the showers bummed by queers,
Ten more years and no parole,
Now he has a sore arsehole!

Cash's tie-less look backfired when he was refused entry to the club.

## ▦ CELTIC ATTACK MURRAY

Something approaching the ultimate in bad taste has to be Celtic's chant that mocks the former Rangers chairman David Murray. Murray, who lost both his legs in a serious car crash in the seventies, was the target of the following chant, sung to the tune of 'We're on the March With...' (the reference to 'the Bouncy' is from a popular Rangers chant where fans sing 'Bouncy, bouncy, bouncy, bouncy, la la la la la la' while jumping up and down):

Who's that lying by the seaside?
Who's that lying by the shore?
David Murray and his wife, 'cos he's paralysed for life.
Oh, he won't be doing the bouncy anymore.
We've got Larsson, we've got Lubo,
David Murray's shite at judo!

## ▦ VILLA ADD INSULT TO INJURY

Some chants are so provocative that arrests have been made as a direct result of their being aired in public. This was the case shortly after Arsenal's Croatian striker Eduardo was badly injured in a match by Birmingham's Martin Taylor. The player broke his leg and fractured his ankle and didn't play again for a year – there were even initial fears that his career might be over.

A week later, Aston Villa visited the Emirates Stadium and their fans showed not an inkling of sensitivity with the following chants, which earned them a public rollicking from both Villa boss Martin O'Neill and Arsenal's Arsène Wenger. Such was the level of anger at the offensive songs that fighting broke out between rival fans, one man was hospitalised and 12 arrests were made. The first song was chanted to the tune of 'Volare' and the second was a reference to The Automatic's 'Monster':

Eduardo, woah-oh,
Eduardo, woah-oh,
He used to have silky skills,
Now he walks like Heather Mills

What's that coming out of your sock?
Is it an ankle? Is it an ankle?

## ▦ FANS' FOOT-IN-MOUTH CHANT

In 2001, an outbreak of foot-and-mouth disease swept British farms, leading to the slaughter and mass incinerations of thousands of cattle. Not a particularly interesting piece of information in relation to this book, you may think. However, Welsh fans, and supporters of other countryside-based clubs, came in for a lot of stick from visiting fans.

It's one thing being accused of bestiality by visiting fans chanting 'Sheepshaggers' but it's quite another to listen to the following song to the tune of 'Bread of Heaven':

> Did the farmers,
> Did the farmers,
> Did the farmers burn your wives?
> Did the farmers burn your wives?

## ANY FERGUSON WILL DO FOR LEEDS

Leeds fans' animosity to Man United knows no bounds and, even when the club found themselves outside of the English top flight, they still found a way to torment their foes. During a League One match against Peterborough, managed by United gaffer Sir Alex Ferguson's son Darren, Leeds fans used 'Tom Hark' to sing this simple but effective song to the opposition manager:

> Your dad's a c*nt and so are you!

## LEEDS' FATHERS' DAYS NIGHTMARE

However, their animosity to all things Man United – even the offspring of their rivals – soon caught Leeds fans out. In 2010, the club had both Kasper Schmeichel and Alex Bruce on their books and there were many matches that featured the pair in the starting line-up. Kasper's father Peter helped United to Premier League dominance in the nineties while Alex's father Steve was instrumental in sparking United's renaissance – neither name was particularly pleasing to the ears of the Elland Road faithful.

Realising their dilemma, the Leeds fans arrived with an amended version of the chant they sang to Ferguson Junior, as follows:

> Your dad's a c*nt but you're all right!

# ANDY GRAY

**Famous to millions as the Sky Sports-turned-talkSPORT pundit, Andy Gray enjoyed a magnificent playing career, starring up front for the likes of Wolves, Everton and Aston Villa.** The Scottish international scored nearly 200 goals and grappled with hundreds of defenders during his career, and that's the subject which gives rise to his favourite chant.

'I like the song that Liverpool fans sing about Gary McAllister [to the tune of "Hooray Hooray, It's a Holi-Holiday"], it's very funny:

> Gary Mac, Gary Mac,
> Gary, Gary Mac,
> He's got no hair but we don't care
> Gary, Gary Mac!

'But my favourite is from my playing days. I used to come up against a defender called Jim Holton who played for Coventry and Man United.'

Holton was a rugged centre-back, who put everything into every game and was a hero to many fans of the teams he played for. But he was no shrinking violet on the pitch as Gray recalls: 'He got me a few times. Let's just say he was rather uncompromising on more than one occasion. The fans used to sing a song about him, which I still remember today':

> Six foot two
> Eyes of blue
> Jim Holton's after you!
> Na na na na na na na na

(The song was popular on the terraces during the seventies as a pastiche of the twenties song 'Has anybody seen my gal?' which began with the lyrics, 'Five foot two, eyes of blue'.)

Andy Gray was the first footballer to use Sure before matches.

# 6

# 'GET YOUR FATHER'S GUN'

**B**ritish football's greatest rivalries – and even some of the worst ones – are steeped in tradition, history and cultural significance. Because passions never run higher than when mortal enemies are involved, perhaps these clashes have helped nurture some of the finest and most original examples of chanting. Be warned, though. This chapter is not big and not clever, but it is undeniably amusing. Here's to football hatred and the wonderful terrace humour it has conjured up over the years.

# ▒ RANGERS v CELTIC

It's difficult to print most of the chants between these two great Glaswegian rivals without offending anyone of a religious persuasion. So, to paraphrase a famous news announcement, if you still believe in god, look away now...

## The Sash

One of the traditional protestant anthems attached to Rangers is 'The Sash', which is an old song that recalls the victories won by King William III in 17th century Ireland. The original song celebrates the Orange sash worn by the protestant armies in battle and the lyrics of the chorus are as follows:

> It is old but it is beautiful, its colours they are fine,
> It was worn at Derry, Aughrim, Enniskillen and the Boyne.
> My father wore it as a youth in the bygone days of yore.
> And it's on the twelfth I long to wear, the Sash my Father wore

Anyone would imagine singing a song like that is incendiary enough given the religious animosity that exists between the clubs, but Rangers fans created a new chorus, paying tribute to the original, but bringing the ancient battlegrounds into the modern day football arena:

> It is old but it is beautiful, it's red, it's white and it's blue,
> It's worn on the slopes of Ibrox Park and a place called Parkhead too.
> My father wore it as a youth in the bygone days of yore.
> And it's on display every Saturday, every time the Rangers score!

## Pants To That

Naturally, Celtic have dozens of their own anti-Rangers songs which play on the religious divide, but they're also capable of more up-to-date chants. Former Rangers' midfielder Charlie Adam was the target for one of the best of these. Using an old Manchester City chant for Niall Quinn to the tune of 'Stars and Stripes Forever', the Celts made up this beauty:

> Charlie Adam's sister's pants are the best,
> You can smell them from the east to the west,
> They are better when soiled and damp,
> Charlie Adam's sister's pants!

# ⠿ DUNDEE v DUNDEE UNITED

Staying in Scotland, rivalries exist beyond the borders of Glasgow as this chant sung by Dundee fans to Dundee United shows. The United fans are known as Weegies which, let's just say, is not a complimentary term in that part of the world. The Dundee regulars sing this one to the tune of 'You Are My Sunshine':

> You are a weegie,
> A smelly weegie,
> You're only happy on giro day,
> Your mum's out stealing,
> Your dad's out dealing,
> Please don't take my hubcaps away!

# ⠿ MORTON v KILMARNOCK

Greenock Morton's traditional rivals are St Mirren, but this chant actually marks the club's rivalry with Kilmarnock. The two clubs have been in different divisions for long enough to dilute any hatred between them, but the song, to the tune of 'Coming Round the Mountain', suggests otherwise:

> We're not the Killie, we're the Ton,
> We're not the Killie, we're the Ton,
> Singing we're not the Killie,
> We're not that fucking silly,
> We're not the Killie, we're the Ton!

# ⠿ ASTON VILLA v BIRMINGHAM

### Circus Tricks

The West Midlands clubs have a bitter rivalry dating back almost as long as English association football itself. But this song first appeared during the nineties when the Blues had fallen on tough times. Barry Fry was manager at St Andrews and Karren Brady, currently starring in *The Apprentice*, first started working in football as the club's managing director.

A spell outside of the top two divisions had led Villa fans to mock their neighbours and the rollercoaster nature of Birmingham's fortunes was summed up in this song that could be heard around Villa Park to the tune of 'Heads, Shoulders, Knees and Toes'. The song is unique in that it is the only football chant to have a penultimate line in which all fans singing pretty much do their own thing before somehow managing to sing the last line in unison:

> There's a circus in the town, in the town,
> Barry Fry is a clown, is a clown
> And Karren Brady is a fucking slaaaaaaaaaag
> [elongated for 10-15 seconds],
> And the Blues are going down, going down!

## Singing The Blues

It may not be on quite the same scale as Villa's old song – mainly due to the lack of ambitious young females on the Villa Park board – but Birmingham have their own simple anti-Villa song. Although they used the old Cockney favourite 'Roll Out the Barrel' as their tune, this song is pure West Midlands in its simplicity and effectiveness:

> Shit on the Villa,
> Shit on the Villa tonight,
> Shit on the Villa,
> Shit on the Villa tonight,
> Shit on the Villa,
> Shit on the Villa tonight,
> Everybody shit on the Villa,
> Cos they're a load of shite!

# ▦ MAN UNITED v LIVERPOOL

## Slumming It

Arguably the biggest rivalry in English football almost certainly has the biggest and best chants – with United supplying most of them.

When proud Liverpudlian activist Pete McGovern wrote the lyrics for 'In My Liverpool Home' he could never have imagined his song being twisted to such devastating effect by United fans. The song was made popular by folk band The Spinners with its opening lines: 'I was born in Liverpool, down by the docks; My religion was Catholic; occupation – hard knocks.' But years later the song could be heard at Old Trafford, sung by Liverpool's most bitter rivals – although this time the lyrics were very different.

United's version has had many verses added over the years but the following represents the lines that are most commonly sung:

In your Liverpool slums,
You look in the dustbin for something to eat,
You find a dead rat and you think it's a treat,
In your Liverpool slums.
In your Liverpool slums,
You shit on the carpet, you piss in the bath,
You finger your grandma, and think it's a laugh,
In your Liverpool slums.
In your Liverpool slums,
You speak in an accent exceedingly rare,
You wear a pink tracksuit and have curly hair,
In your Liverpool slums.
In your Liverpool slums,
Your mum's on the game and your dad's in the nick,
You can't get a job 'cos you're too fucking thick,
In your Liverpool slums

## Hungry For Success

Continuing with their theme of starving Scousers, United also doctored the lyrics of one of the biggest hit singles of all time to poke fun at Liverpool – or the 'bin-dippers' as they refer to them.

Like Pete McGovern above, Bob Geldof must scarcely believe how his song – 'Do They Know It's Christmas?' – written to raise money for starving Ethiopians, has become an Old Trafford festive period favourite. From the beginning of every December until shortly after new year, the Stretford End and the rest of the Theatre of Dreams delight in singing the following again and again:

Feed the Scousers,
Let them know it's Christmas time!

## Signing On The Dotted Line

'You'll Never Walk Alone' also received the treatment – although this chant is sung by football fans across the country. The famous Liverpool anthem, originally from the Rogers and Hammerstein musical *Carousel* was later adopted by the Anfield club after being performed by Gerry and the Pacemakers in 1963.

With unemployment spiralling out of control in the 1980s, and Merseyside particularly badly affected, it wasn't long before United, and many of Liverpool's visiting supporters were singing this chorus instead:

> Sign on, sign on,
> With a pen in your hand,
> 'Cos you'll never get a job,
> You'll never get a job!

## Keeping It Simple

Sometimes, cleverly twisting existing lyrics to arrive with a new terrace anthem is just a bit too much like hard work. When United stalwart Gary Neville came out with a series of provocative comments about Liverpool and celebrated a late Old Trafford winning goal against the old enemy right in front of the visiting fans, a simple chant was composed in his honour. To the tune of 'London Bridge is Falling Down', they still sing:

Seconds later, the shirt was shredded, Neville bulked up and turned green.

Gary Neville is a red,
Is a red,
Is a red,
Gary Neville is a red,
He hates Scousers!

## Making A Mug of Macca

Back in the eighties when Man United played second fiddle to Liverpool, Steve McMahon was one of the Anfield club's key players. A tough midfielder who never gave anything less than the footballing cliché of 110 per cent, McMahon also found himself the unwanted subject of a United chant, to the tune of 'Quartermaster's Store':

He's bald, he's Scouse,
He'll rob your fucking house,
Steve McMahon, Steve McMahon!

## Vidic's Torres Afternoon

Perhaps it's because they're busy using the pens in their hands for signing on, or possibly just creating new anthems for the Kop, but Liverpool don't have many original anti-Man United chants. Of course, there are usual numbers like 'Who the fuck are Man United' to the tune of 'Glory Glory Hallelujah' and 'Manchester is full of shit' to the tune of 'When the Saints Go Marching In', but these are hardly original compositions. Generally speaking, Liverpool tend to sing songs in support of their own team and players rather than against their rivals.

However, the other Reds did come up with an excellent chant aimed at United's Serbian defender Nemanja Vidic, who endured a torrid afternoon at the hands of Fernando Torres during a 4-1 home defeat in 2009.

United fans normally sing the following to the tune of 'Volare':

Nemanja, woah-oh,
Nemanja, woah-oh,
He comes from Serbia,
He'll fucking murder ya!

However, that afternoon, a new chant was born in the away end as the Liverpool fans turned a United song on its head for once:

Torres's old 'Drop and give me ten' trick had worked a treat on Vidic.

Nemanja, woah-oh,
Nemanja, woah-oh,
He comes from Serbia,
And Fernando murdered ya!

## ▦ MAN UNITED v MAN CITY

### Sign of the Times

United's other great rivalry is, of course, with their 'noisy neighbours' Man City. The phrase was coined by Sir Alex Ferguson after City's takeover by the insanely rich Sheikh Mansour bin Zayed al Nahyan gave the club unprecedented spending power, meaning they became genuine title rivals to United. Ferguson was moved to make the comment following the controversy over Carlos Tevez – who joined City from United after the Old Trafford club had failed to take up the option to make his loan deal a permanent move.

To mark the signing, City took out billboards featuring Tevez with the provocative message 'Welcome to Manchester' – reigniting the age-old argument between the clubs suggesting Manchester United shouldn't even take the city's name as they are technically based in Salford.

During the time when it was unclear whether Tevez would remain at United, their fans had been imploring Ferguson to keep the popular striker by singing:

> Fergie, sign him up,
> Fergie, Fergie, sign him up!

But City turned the tables on their rivals the following season, when Tevez scored twice for them in a League Cup semi-final against United and the City of Manchester Stadium fans produced a deafening ironic chorus of their own:

> Fergie, sign him up,
> Fergie, Fergie, sign him up!

## The Tevez U-Turn

Naturally, as a former United player, Tevez was subjected to vile chants from the fans to whom he would eventually become a hero. One particularly cruel chant which City used to sing made light of the Argentinian's scars which he received after being accidentally scalded by boiling water as a child. The City fans used 'When Johnny Comes Marching Home (Again)' (Liverpool's Fernando Torres song) to vent their fury at Tevez:

> His neck scars prove he's lost his head,
> Tevez, Tevez,
> He'll never get a sexy bird,
> Tevez, Tevez,
> You ugly twat, you Argy c*nt,
> They've sewn your head on back to front,
> Carlos Tevez, Herman Munster's head!

The chant became a firm favourite with City fans, but they suddenly had a problem when the Argentine became one of their own. Fortunately, the ever-present resourcefulness of football fans was there to save the day and some inspired – and hastily rewritten – new lyrics were found:

We used to have a song for you,
Tevez, Tevez,
But now you've gone from red to blue,
Tevez, Tevez,
We're sorry for the hurtful words,
I bet you've shagged a load of birds,
Carlos Tevez,
City till he dies

## Barren Run

Perhaps because Liverpool have been a bigger on-pitch threat to United over the years than City, the Old Trafford club don't tend to have as many anti-City songs. While their neighbours can boast dozens, United fans have been content to remind City how long it is since they've won silverware.

Until City's 2011 FA Cup success (which was made all the sweeter by beating United in the semi-final), the Blue half of Manchester had not enjoyed a major trophy since 1976. And that proved to be a source of great amusement to United fans, who would sing the following, to the tune of 'Tom Hark', and change the number of years as appropriate:

In '76, this is true,
A trophy was won by a team in blue,
It's been a long time, since the day,
So we'll sing a song that they fucking hate,
35 years (fuck all)
35 years (fuck all)

## Spelling It Out

More recently, United have also started to sing an even simpler version of 'This Old Man' as an anti-City chant. It may not be big and it may not be clever but it's certainly effective:

U, N, I, T, E, D,
United are the team for me,
With a knick-knack paddy-whack
Give a dog a bone
Why don't City fuck off home?

## Show Me The Money

But City managed to doctor that chant with one of their own to rile the
Old Trafford regulars. As City's financial plight improved with the takeover,
United's worsened under the debt that was piled onto the club by the Glazer
family. This led to the famous 'green and gold' protest movement by United
fans – but also led to City fans rejoicing in their rivals' misfortune:

U, N, I, T, E, D,
That spells fucking debt to me,
With a knick-knack paddy-whack
Give a dog a bone
Ocean Finance on the phone!

## Calypso Kings

One of the oldest football songs was also revived by United fans in the
seventies and has since become an anthem for the anti-Glazer, green and
gold movement. Trinidadian Edric Connor recorded the 'The Manchester
United Calypso' in 1956, with its chorus going as follows:

Manchester,
Manchester United.
A bunch of bouncing Busby Babes,
They deserve to be knighted.
If ever they're playing in your town,
You must get to that football ground.
Take a look and you will see,
Football taught by Matt Busby

United fans still chanted the song on the terraces although they added
their own verse about City's Colin Bell to follow on from the chorus:

Down on Maine Road's greasy pastures
Play a load of dozy bastards,
Colin Bell, the City ace,
A ruptured duck has got more pace!

# ▦ TOTTENHAM v ARSENAL

## Berbatov Hits The Road

The north London rivalry between Tottenham and Arsenal has thrown up plenty of controversy in recent times, particularly when Sol Campbell moved between the clubs. He was subject to plenty of abuse from Spurs fans for his perceived treachery, maintaining a long tradition of each set of fans singing hostile chants about opposition players.

The Arsenal fans were no angels themselves and, years later, they came up with a particularly imaginative, not to mention racially questionable, chant about Tottenham's Bulgarian striker Dimitar Berbatov to the tune of Liverpool's, er, 'Li-ver-pool, Li-ver-pool':

> Di-mi-tar, Di-mi-tar,
> His mum washes cars
> On the North Cir-cu-lar

## Long-Range Effort

In the mid-nineties Spurs fans were experiencing something of a drought on the trophy front and had to resort to taking pleasure from the failures of their great rivals. One of their most popular chants involved remembering a goal scored by one of their former players against Arsenal – a highly unusual premise for a terrace tune. But this was also a highly unusual goal.

Holders Arsenal had enjoyed another run to the final of the European Cup-Winners' Cup in 1995 where they faced Real Zaragoza, who included former Spurs man Nayim among their line-up. The match was heading for a penalty shoot-out when, with seconds remaining, the former Tottenham midfielder lashed a 40-yard shot over Arsenal's England goalkeeper David Seaman to win the cup. Nayim celebrated, Spain celebrated, one half of north London celebrated.

For many years following that game, Spurs fans would always taunt their rivals with this simple chant to the tune of 'Go West':

> Nayim from the halfway line!

## Spurs Look Off Colour

But Arsenal still have a chant they hold dear as it references how long it's been since their rivals last won a league title. Instead of counting the number of years like Man United do for Man City, the Gooners have a much more subtle approach, singing the following to 'Oh When the Saints':

You won the league in black and white,
You won the league in black and white,
You won the league in the sixties,
You won the league in black and white!

Even when relaxing in the garden at home, Danny Blanchflower always wore full kit.

## ▦ NEWCASTLE v SUNDERLAND

### Monkey Business

Just like Carlos Tevez above, you can't be active in the world of professional football, have something distinctive about your facial features and expect to get away with it.

And so, as former England midfielder Peter Reid aged, the more simian his visage became until he began to resemble the missing link in Darwin's theory of evolution.

Unfortunately for him, he happened to be (a fairly successful) manager of Sunderland at the time – and that meant the Newcastle fans had noticed his ape-ish ways.

One of the most famous songs of the nineties was thus born in St James' Park's Gallowgate end, to the tune of 'Yellow Submarine'. The song works far better when you consider that the Geordies pronounce head as 'heed'...

> In the land, where I was born
> Lives a man with a monkey's head
> And he went to Sunderland
> And his name is Peter Reid.
> Peter Reid's got a fucking monkey's head,
> A fucking monkey's head,
> A fucking monkey's head

## Spelling It Out

Weirdly, one of Sunderland's most popular anti-Geordie numbers is a Newcastle song in itself – although admittedly the closing verses of the song are not sung at St James' Park. But, Sunderland – or the Mackems as they're known by their rivals – are hardly singing it in praise of the enemy. Nevertheless, if a passer-by was to hear the beginning of the song, other than the red-and-white shirted masses singing it, there would be nothing to suggest this wasn't a Newcastle chant:

> With an N and an E and a WC
> An A and an S and a T L E,
> U N I T E D,
> Newcastle United fuck off!
> Fuck right off you black and white bastards!

# ▦ CARDIFF v SWANSEA

## Cardiff Do Know Jack

The South Wales derby is as passionate as any, and recently it has seen the clubs fighting for promotion to the Premier League, with Swansea just pipping their rivals to the post in 2011. Cardiff fans claim Swansea take the rivalry more seriously, yet the Bluebirds still sing this song about their neighbours, to the tune of 'In My Liverpool Home':

He's a Swansea Jack,
He's a Swansea Jack,
He wears black and white like he's some sort of queer,
He can't handle women, he can't handle beer,
He's a Swansea Jack

## Swansea Take The Plunge

Since 1988, Swansea have always sung the chorus of 'The Lions Sleeps Tonight' at Cardiff fans, changing the words to 'swim away'. This refers to an incident after that season's Vetch Field derby when Swansea fans chased Cardiff fans through the city and, literally, into the sea – from where police eventually managed to force the Swansea contingent to leave before the Cardiff supporters would emerge from the water.

The Swansea players have even got in on the act, with Darren Pratley celebrating a 2008 derby goal by doing the breaststroke to the delight of the home fans. Recently, a verse was added to accompany the chorus, as follows:

In the Channel,
The Bristol Channel,
The scummers swim tonight.
The water's freezing,
The scum are sneezing,
They'd rather swim than fight…

## ▦ WOLVES v WEST BROM

## Focused And Simple

Until it was banned from derby matches out of fear that it incited violence, the Molineux PA system would play 'The Liquidator' – an instrumental reggae tune popular among skinheads since the seventies. In between each blast of the 'chorus', Wolves fans scream at the tops of their voices:

Fuck off West Brom! The Wolves!

The West Brom retort is marginally more sophisticated, with the Baggies singing the following to the tune of 'Son of My Father'

> Oh Wanky, Wanky,
> Wanky, Wanky, Wanky, Wanky Wanderers!

## ▦ IPSWICH v NORWICH

### The Family Way

One chant that has become ubiquitous as a song that is chorused by fans visiting any footballing outpost is 'The Norwich Family'. Performed to the sounds of *The Addams Family* TV theme tune, the chant was first sung by Ipswich to smear their great rivals with the traditional stains of inbreeding.

Many versions exist, with different team names being replaced in the last line, but this remains the original:

> Your sister is your mother,
> Your uncle is your brother,
> You all fuck one another,
> The Norwich family.
> Der der der der! (clap clap)
> Der der der der! (clap clap)
> Der der der der!
> Der der der der!
> Der der der der!
> (clap clap)

## ▦ BURNLEY v BLACKBURN

### Rovers Lord It Over Clarets

Back in the seventies, Blackburn used to target the chairman of their Lancashire rivals Burnley for their derby song. At the time, the Clarets chairman was Bob Lord, a forthright local businessman who had made money from his butchery business. Lord was no stranger to controversy and was loathed by many in the game – especially Rovers fans, who sang this to the tune of 'My Old Man's A Dustman':

Bob Lord, he was a butcher, he wore a butcher's hat
And when he wore it back to front he looked a fucking twat.
Bob Lord he was a butcher, he made some meat pies,
He gave them to the Scumley fans and half the bastards died

## Burnley Always Say Never

As well as the usual chants sung to rivals, Burnley also have a song that focuses on Blackburn's greatest benefactor. Jack Walker's millions helped transform Blackburn, as they became Premier League champions in 1995 – much to the disgust of Clarets fans, who sing this song to the tune of 'No Nay Never' (there are three verses in total, one is included here):

I went to the alehouse I often frequent,
I saw old Jack Walker his money was spent,
He asked me to play,
I answered him nay,
With rubbish like yours I can beat any day.
And it's no nay never,
No nay never no more,
Till we play bastard Rovers,
No never no more
We hate Bastards!
We hate Bastards!
We hate Bastards!

# ▦ DERBY v LEEDS

## If You Know Your History

Not so much a geographical rivalry as a historical one, Derby retain an animosity towards Leeds which goes back to the seventies when the sides were the best in the country. Don Revie was the Leeds boss while Brian Clough was performing miracles at the Baseball Ground and the pair clashed on several occasions, fuelling the bad feeling between the clubs and their fans.

As such, even three decades later, Derby fans composed this chant after Leeds, managed by Dennis Wise at the time, were relegated to League One (to the tune of 'Lord of the Dance'):

The pre-match toss of the coin had turned particularly nasty.

Wise, Wise whatever have you done,
You've put Leeds in Division One,
You won't win a cup,
You won't win a shield,
Your biggest game will be Huddersfield!

## OXFORD v SWINDON

### Hard Times

The 'A420 derby' between Oxford United and Swindon Town is alive and kicking although both sides have fallen on harder times in recent years. That doesn't mean they still don't sing about each other, and Oxford (who traditionally play in yellow home shirts) chant this to the tune of 'London Bridge is Falling Down':

Swindon town is falling down,
Falling down,
Falling down,
Swindon town is falling down,
Fuck off Swindon!

Build it up with yellow and blue,
Yellow and blue,
Yellow and blue,
Build it up with yellow and blue,
Fuck off Swindon!

## ⠿ ROCHDALE v BURY

### Not Quite A Classic

This may not be a rivalry that rolls off the tongue like Barcelona v Real
Madrid, but it's certainly worthy of mention due to Rochdale's unique
anti-Bury chant. Not many fans would swear at, and insult, themselves in
a chant – certainly not one about their rivals – but that's exactly what the
Dale hardcore do in this gem.

Note to those of southern persuasion: This chant sounds far more
effective using the northern annunciation of bastard than the soft southern
one. It's sung to the tune of 'Oh My Darling, Clementine':

I'm a bastard,
I'm a bastard,
I'm a bastard, yes I am,
But I'd rather be a bastard, than a fucking Bury Fan!

## ⠿ SHEFFIELD UNITED
## v SHEFFIELD WEDNESDAY

### A Flying Visit

The propensity to use children's songs as themes for football chants is
probably due to making sure everyone will know the tune – but it's still
disconcerting to hear an innocent tune corrupted. Not that Sheffield United
fans will be remotely concerned when they use the ditty for 'My Bonnie Lies
Over the Ocean' to target their cross-town rivals.

In truth, this song is used by quite a few teams but given that Sheffield
as a city boasts the world's oldest ever football team (Sheffield FC, 1857) it's
only fair that it takes the honours:

If I had the wings of a sparrow,
The dirty great arse of a crow,
I'd fly over Hillsborough tomorrow,
And shit on the bastards below, below.
Shit on, Shit on,
Shit on the bastards below, below,
Shit on, Shit on,
Shit on the bastards below!

## Living In The Past

Another United favourite is their '1889' chant, which celebrates the year the club was formed. The chant, sung to the tune of American anthem 'Home on the Range', is a nostalgic look back at how life was then for Blades fans – although clearly nobody singing it today has any idea what life was like then – as they sing about Wednesday not having moved to Hillsborough yet.

The reference to pigs is the term used by the rival fans to describe each other, although legend has it Wednesday were first called pigs by United fans when it was discovered that part of the land on which Hillsborough was built was once a pig farm.

No pig fans in town,
No Hillsborough to sadden my eyes,
Jack Charlton is dead,
And the pig fans have fled,
And the year is 1889

## Winding (Up) Lane

Aside from the usual 'Stand up if you hate... ' chants that all rivals sing at each other, Wednesday's response is fairly clinical. Referring to Bramall Lane, where United play, the Hillsborough fans couldn't have spent more than around 10 seconds conjuring up this tuneless classic:

At the Lane, At the Lane,
Where they're all fucking wankers at the Lane!
At the Lane, At the Lane,
Where they're all fucking wankers at the Lane!

# MATT HOLLAND

**Former Ipswich, Charlton and Ireland international Matt Holland was a highly competent midfielder who won a lot of fans with his committed and industrious performances.** Unfortunately those fans never quite came up with a solid signature tune for him: 'My chants were a bit boring really,' says Holland. 'Fans used to sing things like "One Matt Holland".

Weirdly, the life-size table football player had made it onto the pitch.

'When I was playing it was very hard to hear the fans sing as I was always completely in the zone. Sometimes, you don't even realise a substitution was made until the end of the game. Now and again when there's a break in play for a corner or a free-kick, you do hear more what the crowd are singing.

'When I was at Ipswich, I really liked the chant the fans sang for Finidi George, the Nigerian international:

> Finidi, woah-oh,
> Finidi, woah-oh,
> He comes from Africa,
> He drives a big tractor!

'But I'm a Man United fan and my favourite chants are the Ji-Sung Park and Nemanja Vidic ones. I like the humour, particularly in the Park one, although it is quite near the knuckle in terms of Korean culture. As a fan, that is the funniest one.'

[For the full chant go to page 128.]

# 7

# THE EVOLUTION OF THE FOOTBALL CHANT

Since the days of the cavemen, most gatherings of men have tended to result in a sing-song. But how did we arrive at the point where going to the match and singing is all part of the experience? With the help of a few experts, and a genuine bona fide chant writer, this chapter will attempt to explain how football fans went from 'suited and cloth-capped gentle folk' to people who sing 'the referee's a wanker' without so much as a second thought.

# ▦ DEVELOPING FAN CULTURE

The 'club anthems' section of this book provides several examples of early indicators which hint that singing at football has been commonplace since around the 1920s. And even before that, there is evidence of singing being part of the match-day experience. 'I've found examples of singing among Liverpool supporters which go back to at least 1906, which is very early,' explains football sociologist John Williams of Leicester University, who has written several books on the history of Liverpool FC.

'You can see signs of a real creative culture. It is an early feature of the club's support which certainly has its roots in Irish traditions and the working class, aural culture of the city. That was part of the club and became mythologised when the Kop was built and became known as a special place.'

These early examples were not chants as we know them today, but were the roots of fan culture, as supporters united by a common cause would sing together, normally the popular songs of the day. When marching bands provided the entertainment before matches and during half-time, there are also records of supporters singing along to whichever tunes were being

Mrs Green was sunbathing in the dress which showed a glimpse of ankle again.

blasted out by the cornets and drums. West Ham's 'I'm Forever Blowing Bubbles' is a song which was born out of this era, while Cardiff's 'I'll Be There' is a mining song sung at Ninian Park in the 1920s as fans were united by another common cause – most of them would have been pit workers as well as Bluebirds supporters. '"Blaydon Races", sung by Newcastle, shows the fans' working-class roots,' says Professor Mike Weed of Kent University. 'People sing about their backgrounds so localism is important.'

And, of course, there's the self-styled 'oldest football song in the world' sung by Norwich fans ever since football was played in the city. 'On the ball City' is certainly proof that fans have been singing at matches for a long time.

## ▦ SINGING OR SWINGING?

As society opened itself up and cultural norms began to develop, singing at football followed suit. 'In the early sixties, pop music helped to delineate older and younger cultures,' says Williams. 'There's a great *Panorama* film with footage from 1964 where you can see people on the Kop singing the "Merseybeat" songs of the era.'

From there, it was only a matter of time until football fan culture began to express itself in different ways and, as the football chants as we know them today began to be heard, so the ugly spectre of football hooliganism also arose.

Fortunately, chanting at grounds managed to separate itself from the violence, leading to today's situation where rival fans can exchange chants in a ground without necessarily resorting to violence. However, there have been occasions where police have had to intervene. As documented in the 'Get Your Father's Gun' chapter, Wolves stopped playing 'The Liquidator' before matches against West Brom at Molineux because fans would work themselves into such a state while screaming 'Fuck off West Brom! The Wolves!' that the authorities considered it as inciting violence.

Similarly, there has been huge controversy over sectarian chanting at games between Rangers and Celtic in Scotland, with many songs being outlawed. Likewise, as society has entered a more enlightened era, racist and homophobic chanting has also become banned, with the majority of fans backing such moves.

## ▓ SING WHEN YOU'RE WINNING

So, here we are, at the stage where fans can sing and chant almost anything they like – and regularly do – but how does this actually work in practice and why do so many people join in? 'Supporters are part of the event themselves, they help to create it and singing is partly about that,' says Williams. 'Fans are not just participants, they're actors, people who are involved, who can help swing the tide of matches. They're now encouraged by managers and players to support well and get involved because it supports the players.

'And the data now on the number of home wins versus away wins shows that the support may have a positive impact on the performance of the team. The sense of being a player and part of the event is a key feature of why people sing.'

This is a crucial point as supporters are regularly reminded of the role they play, almost to the extent of being made to feel guilty if they're not vocal enough.

Before their Champions League quarter-final against Chelsea in 2011, Man United manager Sir Alex Ferguson issued this plea in the match programme: 'When we get to the nitty-gritty stage of a competition, our fans always respond. The volume from the crowd goes up, and all the players will tell you that it helps enormously. I'm banking on you. I ask you to make Old Trafford a cauldron of noise this evening.'

It was an amazing turnout for the new Anfield groundsman's first seeding shift.

And from 75,000 screaming fans to 3,000 doing their utmost to shout themselves hoarse, all support is vital as shown by this message from Walsall manager Dean Smith ahead of a crucial match in the club's 2011 relegation battle: 'The supporters have a massive part to play. They've got behind us and when they've done that it's lifted us. One of the big examples was against Southampton when it was a backs-to-the-walls job and the supporters got involved and pulled us through.'

Ex-professional players would certainly back this point up as well, with former West Ham and England defender Alvin Martin emphasising how much of a difference the support – or abuse – from the crowd can make: 'Fans shouldn't underestimate their influence on a game. It always surprises me that they don't understand how much influence they can have, negative or positive. While a player might not let it show, negativity can make the game really difficult for him.'

Professor Weed also points out that singing and chanting is not just about trying to cheer on the team to three points, because supporters sing miles away from the ground as well: 'Sometimes, it's beyond supporting a team,' he says. 'Chants take place outside the ground, then it's about a demonstration of identity and belonging to a particular group. It's about demonstrating and feeling part of something bigger than yourself; a movement.'

## WHO WRITES THE SONGS?

Even though the so-called 'electric' atmospheres that are regularly described by reporters and visitors to grounds require thousands of participants, it's surprising that most chants emerge from a very small number of people who sing two types of song. Apart from the generic chants that can be found elsewhere in the dictionary section of this book, fans tend to create their own player-and-club specific songs. There is general agreement that this is done in two ways – there are pre-planned songs for the visits of certain teams and players, and then there are the moments when chants suddenly spring up spontaneously.

'The research we've done indicates that chants about current players, or even ones with topical references, tend to emanate from a very small group of people,' explains Professor Weed. 'Over time, people who are known to be a club's chant leaders will have their songs picked up. Whereas somebody not known for that, wouldn't have their songs picked up in that way.'

Williams agrees that there seems to be a set group of people who are responsible for the majority of every club's chants. 'Groups of cultural intermediaries who are known by other people in the supporters' group literally sit and devise songs,' he says. 'They don't always work and they have to be trialled to see whether they make sense to people and whether the rest of the supporters pick them up.'

However, Williams is not so sure that every club is home to such powerful creative sources: 'Certainly in Liverpool, there's a group of people who meet and write songs for new players or a new manager. That definitely goes on. But that's quite unusual as in most places, these chants and songs are learned from others [clubs] and then adapted.'

One of those chant writers is Manchester United fan Pete Boyle, who has been composing songs for his fellow fans for the best part of two decades. He believes sharing the songs with a selected group of supporters is paramount to its chances of catching on: 'The key to it is away games,' he says. 'You get more hardcore, dedicated fans. We sing songs on the coach and in the pubs when we get there. If a song takes off in a big way at an away game then it'll be heard at the home game the following week.'

Modernity has certainly affected football chanting with the internet able to make or break chants before they've even reached the pubs, while also giving fans access to the songs of other clubs. 'We're living in much more fluid and global times now and supporters can see and listen to chants and ways of supporting from right across the globe,' says Williams. 'You can see signs of that across different clubs – Crystal Palace are using a continental chant with different notes and levels ['Dale Cavese' – see the chapter 'It's All Greek To Me']. It's very clear that supporters are learning from each other.'

But Professor Weed is not convinced that the internet is necessarily encouraging chanting creativity. 'What tends to get spread is something that's already happened at a ground,' he says. 'Someone goes online and says "we sang this today". I don't think things like the internet have a particular effect in starting chants, those sorts of things come from people who are established chant leaders in the ground.'

And Boyle agrees, citing the negative impact online forums can have when it comes to trying to establish a chant. 'The internet is a danger. There are all these wannabe songsters who post songs on the internet. And as soon as something half-decent has been posted, someone will write "Oh this line fits better" and so on, and they never take off. I never post in these forums because the songs get butchered.'

**WHO ARE YA?**

Unfortunately for them, while the City fans had their backs turned, the linesman raised his offside flag.

But with the influence of continental European chants being seen increasingly at British grounds, with numbers from St Pauli, Cavese and others doing the rounds, the smaller world in which we all live has certainly had an impact on what was, according to Professor Weed, a unique British chanting culture. 'There are more examples of spontaneous chanting in British football and tailored chants to the opposition team too,' he says. 'On the continent, it tends to be more traditional chants in support of the team but less spontaneous than in the UK.'

But Williams is not entirely certain that British fan culture is so distinct, given the improved stadium facilities and the way it has been influenced by European clubs recently. 'We have a sense that British support is much more participatory, but all-seater stadiums have made it more difficult to participate and now we're learning about different methods of supporting from the continent.

'Man City turning their backs to celebrate a goal is a direct import from one of their European games [against Lech Poznan]. I think there's a lot more merging of styles now. Some people actively go looking for chants and songs on the internet to use them in their own locales. So it's not easy to say there's a definitive British style anymore.

'It's not necessarily a bad thing – I like the Man City thing, it's not original but it symbolises they're back in European competition. There may be a subtext to that particular mode of supporting. There's a lot more exchanging [of chants] so it's much harder to be authentic.'

Professor Weed agrees that the way the Premier League has changed the face of English football has certainly had an impact on the specific nature of the chants that are now sung, with some less politically correct undertones no longer welcome. 'The move towards all-seater stadiums has suppressed some atmosphere, but some abusive chants have still survived. I think in Premier League grounds this sort of behaviour will be less tolerated. Sky don't want to broadcast it either.'

So we could be looking at a future where fans are more likely to sing 'You're not fit to referee' rather than 'The referee's a wanker', meaning chant gurus like Boyle could be forced to rewrite their songbooks – not that he would be concerned as he claims to have written around '400 chants, half of which never took off'. Boyle has even gone as far as writing songs for players yet to sign for United, trying to get ahead of the game by buying into newspaper speculation: 'I once wrote one for [Hristo] Stoichkov and one for Marc Overmars [who went to Arsenal] – they never signed, so I had to shelve them.'

As for which chants are likely to catch on, Boyle is certain there is little science to it, citing the time he tried to start a chant for United supersub Ole Gunnar Solskjaer. 'Some shitter songs I've written have taken off and other better ones have fallen by the wayside,' says Boyle. 'We were at Charlton away in 1999 – we'd beaten Liverpool the week before and Solskjaer had scored the winner. So I was in the pub that day trying to get a Solskjaer song started – it was "Ole Ole Ole Ole, Gunnar Solskjaer" [to the tune of "Hot Hot Hot"] and no one was really singing it.

'I don't like recycling old United songs but in the seventies we used to sing "Who put the ball in the West Ham net? Skip to my Lou Macari." And it just came to me. I hadn't planned it and I started singing "Who put the ball in the Scousers' net? Ole Gunnar Solskjaer." The whole ground sang it for virtually the whole of the game. Sometimes, you try too hard and you prepare too much.'

Fearlessness and shamelessness are both qualities that the potential chant leader has to employ to be able to effectively operate and Boyle has an abundance of both, having had to develop a thick skin over the years if his chants are rejected. 'I don't get embarrassed if people don't join in, I just try another one,' he says. 'Sometimes it's just not meant to be. When we were playing Leeds away in 1999 "Gary Neville is a Red, he hates Scousers" just came into my head and I sung it out loud; everyone loved it.'

# ▦ REBEL YELL OR POETRY IN MOTION?

But, after hearing from academics and a chant writer, it's only fitting that the final word in this discourse on football chanting should come from an officially appointed cultural authority. And who better than the former UK Poet Laureate Sir Andrew Motion?

Shortly before coming to the end of his tenure in 2009, Motion told the *Observer* he was convinced that football chants were works of art: 'Poetry is a simple, primitive thing and, although it's unusual to find football chants being elaborated to the point at which they'll make anything that resembles a poem as we ordinarily understand it, they are an aspect of poetry.'

'Football chanting is a kind of animal, impulsive instinct. They can be bracingly vulgar, but they can often be very funny, and sometimes quite ingenious.'

Next time you're singing your heart out for the lads, feel free to think about how you're spurring your team on, how you're part of a group with a strong identity, how football fans before you have been singing for more than a century. But, most of all, feel free to think about how you're in the same league as Keats, Wordsworth and Byron.

'I'm a Barbie girl, in a Barbie wor-or-old.'

# RAY HOUGHTON

**A magnificent career saw Ray Houghton excel for Oxford, Liverpool and Aston Villa but it was his international exploits for Ireland that saw him worshipped, particularly for two goals.** One was the only goal in a sensational victory against Italy in the 1994 World Cup, but it was the other goal that sparked Houghton's favourite chant.

'My brother actually started my favourite chant. It was about the goal I scored against England at the European Championships in 1988. We were having a bit of a sing-song in the pub after the game with other players and a few fans and my brother started singing (to the tune of 'Camptown Races'):

> Who put the ball in the English net?
> Ray-o! Ray-o!

'And it caught on from there. It's really strange to hear it and I still hear it today wherever I go.'

Houghton's ability to levitate at will gave him a distinct advantage.

# 8

# IT'S ALL GREEK TO ME

There's no doubt that the influence of continental chants is now being felt in British football with many tunes – if not the lyrics – making their way to these shores. Recent examples include the White Stripes' 'Seven Nation Army' and 'When Johnny Comes Marching Home'. Both of these were European staples before they became popular over here. This chapter seeks out what our football fan brethren from around the world sing to amuse themselves while supporting their teams.

# ▦ DUTCH COURAGE

Around any World Cup, see any crowds of orange-shirted football fans and you won't be far from the phrase 'Hup Holland Hup'. The phrase actually forms part of a famous chant which fans of the Dutch national team sing at all their matches. The song was written in 1950 and when translated now seems fairly dated.

It's essentially asking the national team not to embarrass the pride of the Dutch lion when they take to the pitch and is sung to a traditional Dutch tune – somehow, it's unlikely that a version of this will make its way into British grounds at any time soon. But, long live tradition:

> Go Holland Go,
> Don't let the lion stand in his little vest,
> Go Holland Go,
> Don't let the animal wear slippers,
> Go Holland Go,
> Don't let them beat you out of the field,
> Because the lion wearing football boots
> Can take on the whole world

# ▦ SILENT NIGHTS

Another Dutch favourite which can be heard at many grounds across the Netherlands is their equivalent of the British 'You're not singing anymore!' The Dutch version is slightly more literal and is chanted to the tune of the Europop classic 'Go West'. So, next time you're watching Ajax or PSV Eindhoven take the lead against a British side in a European tie and you hear 'Het is stil aan de overkant!' you'll know what they're singing:

> It is silent on the other side!

# ▦ ALL GREEK TO ME

When British fans worship their clubs, it's enough to chant 'We love you [insert name] we do... '; but Greek fans have other ideas. Panathinaikos supporters have a chant called 'Horto Magiko', bellowed like a herd of army drill sergeants, which compares their love for the club to a drug addiction and can sound extremely intimidating for opponents.

This translation probably fails to do it justice but it's still powerful stuff:

It's a magic weed, give me a little bit to taste,
To dream of my Pao and shout as far as god,
My Panatha, I love you, like heroin, like a hard drug,
Like hashish, LSD.
For you Pao, the whole world is stoned (the whole world!),
My Panatha, my Panatha,
I love you (I love you!).
Wherever you may play I will always follow you (I follow you!),
Pao here (Pao here!),
Pao there (Pao there!),
Wherever you may play,
We will always be together (always together!)

## ▦ GREEKS CAMP OUT IN LONDON

Another Greek team, Olympiakos, were not as literate and in touch with their feminine side as Panathinaikos, judging from a chant that was heard in London. Chelsea were hosting the Greeks in a Champions League tie and one of the visiting supporters had certainly learned some rudimentary English as, suddenly, the cool, west London night was soured with this song:

All of you are gays, gays, gays,
All of you are gays, gays, gays,
All of you are gays!

## ▦ CITY OF PEACE?

Like Panathinaikos, Israeli club Beitar Jerusalem has a set of fans who sing love songs to their team – perhaps it's something to do with the proximity to the Mediterranean air and the balmy temperatures. Beitar, who play in yellow and black, have a reputation for aggressive and controversial support and their fans revel in their bad name. Rivalries with Hapoel

This Beitar Jerusalem fan vowed never to trim his moustache until his team won the Champions League.

Tel Aviv and Maccabi Tel Aviv are often enflamed by their chants. This is a good example of one of those love songs, which quickly turns nasty:

> I love you, I love you, I swear, I swear,
> I think of you every minute of the day, anywhere, always.
> Police won't stop me, my heart will always be yellow-black,
> Beitar, I'm with you until the day I die.
> I hate Hapoel, and Maccabi as well,
> Yellow-black in my soul,
> Go Beitar! We want to see you go to war!

And the following chant is a good example of the reverse as Beitar start with the abuse of their rivals but then break out into a passionate declaration of intent – the closest British clubs come to this is '[insert name] till I die':

> I can't stand Haifa,
> I hate Hapoel,
> Maccabi is a whore.
> I love Beitar,
> You'll never fall because we are united,
> Loving only you, we'll give you our soul!

## ▦ WHEAT BEER FOR BAYERN

Despite their famous footballing enmity, German and British football fans are actually very similar in terms of their basic needs. They both love their football and the drinking culture associated with it, and both sing about it too. While the British tend to sing about being 'pissed out of our heads' or 'we are the drunk and disorderly', the Germans are slightly less graphic in their songs as this homage to Bayern Munich shows:

> In the red jerseys we play,
> And we prefer to drink wheat beer,
> For over a hundred years,
> Our flag blows in Germany,
> In the red jerseys we play!

## ▦ YOUNG AND UPSTANDING LEVERKUSEN FANS

But not all German fans are that subtle – in fact, Bayer Leverkusen fans are the complete opposite with their chants about drinking and, er, fornicating. Travelling Bayer fans tend to sing these songs upon arrival in whichever city their team is playing, leaving the locals in no doubt that if they hadn't already locked up their daughters, they better had (the song refers to the City of Colour, which is another name for Leverkusen, a city with a history of dye manufacturing):

> We are the horny young men from the City of Colour,
> Drinking or what?
> Drinking or what?
> We are the horny young men from the City of Colour,
> Fucking or what?
> Fucking or what?

## ▦ LEVERKUSEN GO TO GREAT LENGTHS

There is another Leverkusen song which is a skit on Nena's famous '99 Red Balloons' but this would seem to have been penned by a teenage fan, given its juvenile tone – unless all German men were brought up on Benny Hill.

This particular one talks about '99 sagging breasts flying over Leverkusen', but the less said about that the better.

One more Leverkusen chant sung at away matches is worthy of mention. It focuses on similar themes to the previous one and might explain the paucity of the club's female travelling fans:

> We're from the West,
> We are the best,
> Ours are the longest,
> Everyone else forget it!
> We come from Bayer,
> We have large testicles,
> And we sing Bayer forever!

# ARGIE-BARGY

In Argentina, there is no love lost between Buenos Aires rivals Boca Juniors and River Plate, a derby which makes some British grudge matches seem rather tame. Just as Real Madrid v Barcelona is known as *El Clasico*, so any Boca v River contest is referred to as the *Superclasico*. Dividing lines have long been established along class, with Boca followed by poorer, working-class communities and River attracting more upper-class support.

The fixture has seen one major tragedy, known as 'Puerta 12' or Gate 12, where 71 Boca fans died after a stampede, the cause of which was never officially determined. Today, Gate 12 is home to Boca's most fanatical fans, who sing two passionate songs about their rivals:

> River River, man,
> You bunch of motherfuckers.
> River River, man,
> You bunch of motherfuckers.
> You're always talking shit,
> You're always making promises.
> When you come to the 12,
> You all take off running,
> You all take off running

The new series of *The Krypton Factor* kept the fans extremely close to the action.

The other song is aimed at the perceived fair-weather nature of the River Plate supporters:

> That's how chickens are,
> The bitter one of Argentina.
> When they aren't the champs,
> Their stands are empty.
> I'm from Boca, sir,
> We all sing with joy,
> Even if we aren't the champs,
> My feelings do not end

## LAZIO GO BLUE

Over in Italy, Lazio's fanatics always sing 'Non Mollare Mai' before each game, which means 'Never Give Up', but they also sing a song that is more familiar to British fans. Using a mixture of 'Itanglian' and English they sing their own version of the Chelsea anthem 'Blue is the Colour' – when they're not too busy singing their mixture of anti-Roma, fascist chants that is:

Blue is the colour,
Football is the game,
SS Lazio you'll never walk alone,
Perchè la Lazio noi sosterrem (That's why Lazio we'll always support)
E per sempre canterem la Lazio (And we'll always sing Lazio)

## ▦ ROMA EARN THEIR WHITE STRIPES

Lazio's city neighbours Roma are responsible for the exportation of the 'Seven Nation Army' song across Europe – but they didn't start it. That honour goes to Belgium's FC Bruges, who took on Roma in a UEFA Cup tie in 2006 and sang the song throughout. There were no words, just the guitar riff 'po-po-po-po-po-po-po' repeated, but when Roma took the song back to Italy, they chanted it with their own amendment:

Biancazzurro bastardo!

Quite simply, this means 'Blue and white bastards' and was a reference to their hated rivals, Lazio. The chant caught on and Italian fans sang it as their team marched to World Cup victory in 2006, although this time it was without the bastard reference and included:

Siamo i campioni del mondo (We are the world champions)

## ▦ GAZZA BLOWS HOT AND COLD

It didn't take long for Italian fans to work out that Paul Gascoigne enjoyed the odd tipple. The England midfielder's time at Lazio had highs and lows, much like his entire career, and the Roma fans enjoyed ridiculing their rivals' star signing. It doesn't translate that well to English, but the Roma fans used to sing the following chant to express their feelings about Gazza:

Drunk man with the earring,
Paul Gascoigne make us a blowjob!

## ▦ NO MERCY FOR THE OLD LADY

The Roma ultras also had little time for Juventus, the 'Old Lady' of Italian football, or its fans. One of the most popular chants the Roma supporters sing about Juve refers to the Turin club's fans working at the Fiat factory for the Agnelli family:

Every Monday such a humiliation,
To go to the factory, serving your boss.
Oh, Juventus fan,
Cocksucker,
Of the whole Agnelli family
And Juve shit, Juve Juve shit!

## ▦ THE MAN WHO NEEDS NO INTRODUCTION

Staying in Italy, Napoli fans still sing about Diego Maradona in the same way that Man United fans still chant about Eric Cantona. The difference is that

Maradona had no choice but to challenge the photographer to a fight.

the Napoli chant is far more subtle and is one of a rare type of chant that doesn't even mention the name of the player or the club.

Before Maradona played for them, Napoli had never won the *Scudetto* (the Italian championship), but all that was to change as the Argentine led them to two titles and other trophies, including the UEFA Cup. To say the Napoli fans idolised him and continue to do so is an understatement – in southern Italy, his name is holy. And that's why the words on the banner which is unfurled at every home game are the same as the chant they sing:

I have seen him, now I can die

## ▦ WHEREFORE ART THOU ROMEO?

Mention the name Toto Schillaci and every Englishman goes misty-eyed with thoughts of Italia 90 and what might have been. You'd imagine the same would be true for Italian fans, given that Toto won the Golden Boot as Italy *also* lost a semi-final on penalties.

However, many Italian football fans also associate Schillaci with Alfa Romeos following an embarrassing incident involving his brother, who was once arrested for stealing parts from an Alfa Romeo 33. As a result of that, Schillaci's popular chant in Italy at the time was amended as follows:

There is in Italy,
A player who
Plays football better than Pele.
Toto, Toto Schillaci, Toto Schillaci
There is in Italy,
A player who
Steals the tires from an Alfa 33.
Steals them, Schillaci steals them, Schillaci steals them!

## ▦ THE REFEREE IS GORGEOUS!

There are not many fans who will cheer the opposition and hail the referee no matter what – in fact, the only ones who do are those who loyally follow Spanish strugglers Cadiz. Last seen in La Liga in 2006, the Andalucians are the rarest of football fans in that they will have a good time no matter what. It's hard to imagine a Cadiz fan ringing the Spanish version of *talkSPORT* to complain about the referee costing them points or that the chairman needs to get the chequebook out. So much so that fans drape banners in the stadium which say: 'Referee, you're gorgeous!' and when David Beckham visited with Real Madrid, he was welcomed with kisses blown from the stands as opposed to the usual vitriol that awaited him when he went elsewhere.

The chant that sums up Cadiz fans best of all is one that has become an unofficial anthem for them and is quite beautiful in its simplicity:

> Alcohol, alcohol, alcohol,
> We came here to get drunk,
> And the result doesn't matter at all!

## ▦ VIENNA CALLING

One of the relatively unknown grudge matches of European football is the Vienna derby between Austria and Rapid. Rapid, who wear green and white and play in the Hutteldorf part of Vienna, have been marginally the more successful of the two clubs in terms of league titles, but that hasn't stopped the violet-clad Austria fans from creating some highly enterprising chants about their neighbours. The references to the 'notes at the social office' are aimed at the poorer Rapid fans, who rely on the welfare state to support them:

> And every Monday, you green pigs,
> You stand at the social office to pick up your notes.
> Oh SK Rapid, you sons of bitches,
> We are the Violets and hate you forever!

The Violets also sing an unflattering song about the surrounding area of the Rapid stadium:

> Come on tell it to all the people,
> The shit lives in Hutteldorf.
> Come on tell it to all the people,
> The shit is green and white (and smells like fish)

## ▦ PHILLY DON'T LACK BOTTLE

It seems that our cousins across the pond in the USA have caught on to some of our ironic and topical chanting. When Kansas City were playing Philadelphia Union in a Major League Soccer match recently, the Union's supporters – known as Sons of Ben after the States' founding father Benjamin Franklin who was Philly-born and bred – gave a particularly warm welcome to the visiting coach. Kansas manager Peter Vermes had recently been arrested for 'Driving under the influence' and the Sons of Ben took no pity as they sang *every one* of the 99 verses of the following song:

> 99 bottles of beer on the wall,
> 99 bottles of beer,
> Peter Vermes, give us your keys.
> 98 bottles of beer on the wall...!

## ▦ SINGING THEIR HEARTS OUT

And Toronto FC fans have also adopted a similarly tongue-in-cheek British sense of humour with some of their chanting. One of their fans' staples whenever they have to make a trip into the States for an MLS game is to make fun of the huge lifestyle difficulty faced by Americans who have no state-funded healthcare system. Singing to the tune of 'I Came, I Saw, I Conga'd', the Canadians chant:

> We don't pay for healthcare,
> We don't pay for healthcare,
> La la la la,
> La la la la!

## ▦ BEWARE OF IMITATIONS

Germany's FC St Pauli is a European club which has become famous for adopting a zero-tolerance approach towards right-wing extremism. Their punk-loving left-wing fans regularly create an inspiring atmosphere at matches thanks to their passionate and original chanting.

One of these chants is in English and, as such, has started to become used in lower league football across the UK at clubs like Crystal Palace and Stevenage. So if you start to hear this catchy number at a ground near you soon, remember who was first – St Pauli:

We love you, we love you, we love you,
And when you play we follow, we follow, we follow,
Because we support St Pauli, St Pauli, St Pauli,
And that's the way we like it, we like it, we like it.
Woah-oh-oh-oh woooaaaaahhh,
Woah-oh-oh-oh woooaaaaahhh,
Woah-oh-oh-oh woooaaaaahhh,
Woah-oh-oh-oh woooaaaaahhh
That's the way aha, aha, we like it, aha, aha,
That's the way aha, aha, we like it, aha, aha.
Woah-oh-woah-oh-woah-oh-woah-oh-woah (St Pauli!),
Woah-oh-woah-oh-woah-oh-woah-oh-woah (St Pauli!)

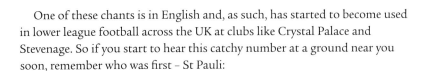

# ▦ DOING THE CAVESE

It's hard to imagine that Venezuela could have influenced European football chanting in any significant way. But it's a little known fact that Caracas-born Hugo Blanco's 'Moliendo Café' is the inspiration behind one of the continent's most contemporary terrace tunes. The popular song became a number one hit in Argentina in 1961 and was subsequently played by the Boca Juniors band with fans accompanying with various 'woah-ohs' and 'na-na-nas' where appropriate.

But, the tune (the chant has no words) really took off when a mightily impressive video of fans of Italian minnows Cavese emerged on the internet, becoming known as 'Dale Cavese' or 'Come on Cavese'.

Pretty soon, fans of clubs from Accrington to Istanbul were imitating the Italians and a new cult chant had been born. Thanks to a Venezuelan.

# ▦ FLOWER OF FRANCE

You would imagine that 'Flower of Scotland' remains unique to those from north of the border – and quite rightly too. Yet, strangely, fans of Paris St Germain have adopted the song's tune to chant their ode to the love of their lives.

The song, which naturally sounds better in French so both versions have been included, is another of those rare ones which doesn't mention the team or players. But, unlike the previous 'Cavese' phenomenon, it does have words:

Oh ville lumière,
Sens la chaleur
De notre coeur,
Vois-tu notre ferveur?
Quand nous marchons près de toi
Dans cette quête
Chasser l'ennemi,
Enfin pour que nos couleurs
Brillent encore

Oh city of lights,
Feel the warmth
In our hearts.
Can you see our fervour?
When we are walking beside you
On this quest
To hunt down the enemy,
So that our colours
Can shine again

# ▦ TAKASHI'S KING OF THE CAST

Clive Tyldesley once famously said 'Wayne Rooney, remember the name,' and Japanese fans of Gamba Osaka are convinced their prodigy Usami Takashi is worthy of similar memory space – Bayern Munich agree as they signed the then 19-year-old in June 2011.

The Osaka fans were probably the world's first to create a football chant to the theme tune of kids' TV cartoon *Popeye* – and they also had the decency to throw in some English words too:

Oh Usami Takashi,
Oh Usami Takashi,
Oh Usami goal, Usami goal,
Usami Takashi, get goal!

# ▦ DIAMONDS ARE FOREVER

And staying in Japan, the supporters of Urawa Red Diamonds also use English to salute their team in an extraordinary way. The club's chanting has now been made famous through internet footage of Diamonds fans singing a Japanese version of 'The Great Escape'. But it's the awe-inspiring 'We Are Diamonds', sung in English and Japanese to the tune of 'We Are Sailing', that is most impressive – particularly when an entire section of the ground joins in to sing as one – the electric atmosphere on a par or better than any famous Anfield European Cup night. They've learned well.

Urawa Red Diamonds fans were just getting to the 'heads' part of 'Head, shoulders, knees and toes'.

# CHRIS KAMARA

**Chris Kamara is now known for his work as a presenter and analyst on Sky Sports with his lively reports on *Soccer Saturday* endearing him to the nation.**

In his playing days, Kamara was a much travelled, no-nonsense centre-half, who first turned out for Portsmouth after a stint in the Royal Navy. 'I grew up on the Pompey Chimes,' he says. 'So that's definitely among my favourite chants. Swindon used to sing the "celery" song and the fans would also turn up to matches with sticks of celery!

'When I played at Stoke, the fans sung "Delilah" which always sounded great, and Leeds doing "Marching on Together" was up there with "You'll Never Walk Alone" and "I'm Forever Blowing Bubbles" as an anthem.

'When I managed Bradford, we got to Wembley and won in the play-offs. The fans chanted "There's only one Chris Kamara, walking in a City wonderland" so I liked that one too!'

But Kamara opts for none of these as his overall favourite, instead making the unlikely choice of 'Que sera, sera': 'I love Doris Day's version of "Que sera sera". I love the song anyway, and I love it when fans sing it about going to Wembley':

> Que sera sera,
> Whatever will be, will be,
> We're going to Wem-ber-lee,
> Que sera sera!

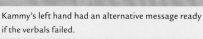

Kammy's left hand had an alternative message ready if the verbals failed.

# CULT
# HEROES

Some players were born not just to play football, but also to be chanted about. And some of them might have been better off just being chanted about rather than playing football. This chapter hails some of the players who have had the most songs composed in their honour – for better or worse – and also those footballers whose chants have added to their cool status due to the originality of their songs. These are our cult heroes...

# ADEBAYOR SLIDES INTO FOLKLORE

As soon as Arsenal first sang their Emmanuel Adebayor chant (to the tune of 'Sloop John B'), a whole host of alternative offensive versions were crafted. But when the striker moved to Man City, fans were waiting for him with plenty more friendly versions.

These were especially enhanced by the first meeting between the Togolese and his former employers, when he scored and ran the length of the pitch to celebrate on his knees in front of his *former* fans. He also found time to stamp on his ex-teammate Robin van Persie during that match, an action for which the FA banned him for three games.

But all that (probably) paled into insignificance when City fans sang:

Adebayor,
Adebayor,
He stamped on Van Persie
And slid on the floor!

Adebayor loved a celebration so much he even went for it in the pre-match kickabout.

## ▦ ADEBAYOR'S FLYING START

The striker's amazing start to life at the City of Manchester Stadium also endeared him to his new fans. He managed to score within three minutes of his debut against Blackburn and notched in each of his first four games.

At the same time, City's rivals United were not getting the best value for money out of their expensive forward Dimitar Berbatov, giving rise to the following City chant:

> Adebayor,
> Adebayor,
> He costs less than Berbatov
> And scores a lot more!

## ▦ ADE-BYE-OR

Despite an excellent first season for City, it wasn't long before stories of dressing room unrest and an uneasy relationship with new manager Roberto Mancini led to rumours of a mid-season departure. And these rumours were fuelled by further speculation that City were poised to make a raid to sign Liverpool's Fernando Torres. Suddenly, City fans were singing Adebayor's name again, but this time the song would not have been to his liking:

> Adebayor,
> Adebayor,
> Once we sign Torres
> He's out of the door!

## ▦ SMALL IS BEAUTIFUL

Arsenal fans still managed to sing their Adebayor song even after the striker's departure. Naturally, the words were amended, as was the object of their affections, with the Emirates Stadium now ringing out to tributes to new signing Andrei Arshavin, the pint-sized Russian forward.

Just to show poetic licence exists in the world of football chanting, the Gunners were slightly inaccurate about the true size of the winger – but his real height of 5ft 8in wouldn't have rhymed:

He's five foot four,
He's five foot four,
We've got Arshavin,
Fuck Adebayor!

## ▦ O'SHEA'S MARCH TO GLORY

When Fernando Torres signed for Liverpool, the Kop had a song ready for him to the tune of 'When Johnny Comes Marching Home'. This led to a spate of copycat songs across English football grounds, but it wasn't the first time it had been used in the country. In fact, it had first been sung in the UK by Liverpool's arch-rivals Manchester United to salute their unsung hero John O'Shea, back in 2002:

When Johnny goes marching down the wing,
O'Shea! O'Shea!
When Johnny goes marching down the wing,
O'Shea! O'Shea!
When Johnny goes marching down the wing,
The Stretford End will fucking sing:
'We all know that Johnny's gonna score'
La, la, la, la, la, la, la, la,
La, la, la, la
La, la, la, la, la, la, la, la,
La, la, la, la,
La, la, la, la, la, la, la, la, la
La, la, la, la, la, la, la, la, la
'We all know that Johnny's gonna score!'

## ▦ LIVERPOOL'S NUMBER NINE

Back to Liverpool where the Torres song became a huge terrace hit, far more so than O'Shea's, arguably because the impact the Spaniard made was far greater than the Irishman's. It was famously revealed that the Atletico Madrid striker had the slogan 'We'll Never Walk Alone' written on the inside of his captain's armband, leading many to the conclusion there was only ever one club he was destined to play for. In fact, this was a pact he had made with friends, who had all been tattooed with the slogan (a popular phrase in Spain), although Torres declined to get the permanent mark made as he didn't want to offend his club due to the phrase's obvious associations with the English team.

However, in 2007 he was to move to Anfield in any case, and the fans took the player to their hearts, with the armband story a huge part of the myth that was created, claiming it was fate that had brought him to Merseyside. And this is the beginning of the song that was composed in his honour:

> His armband proved he was a Red,
> Torres, Torres,
> 'You'll never walk alone' it said,
> Torres, Torres,
> We bought the lad from sunny Spain,
> He gets the ball, he scores again,
> Fernando Torres is Liverpool's number nine!

## ▦ LIVERPOOL SAY ADIOS

Three-and-a-half years later, Torres joined Chelsea for £50 million and thousands of Kop-ites were heartbroken and hurt. His first season at Anfield was extraordinary as he scored 36 goals and looked to be the closest thing to the Second Coming that Liverpool had seen since Kenny Dalglish. But through a combination of injury and a slight decline in form, the goal count lowered over the course of the next two seasons, although by the time he left he still had the hugely impressive statistic of 65 goals in 91 Premier League games for the club.

The Kop were outraged and it wasn't long before an alternative version of their favourite chant had been composed, which also managed a dig at John Terry for good measure:

> His armband lied – he was no red,
> Torres, Torres,
> He's just a rentboy like they said,
> Torres, Torres,

Into our backs he plunged his knife,
I hope John Terry shags his wife,
Fernando Torres, he's just a pile of shite!

## UNITED'S TAWDRY TORRES TRIBUTE

Even prior to Liverpool's new take on their own song, rivals Man United had come up with their own version of the Torres chant. Playing on the Spanish striker's boyish good looks, some United fans began singing this song instead:

He's half a boy, he's half a girl,
Torres, Torres,
He looks just like a transvestite,
Torres, Torres,
He wears a frock, he loves the cock,
He sells his arse on Albert Dock,
Fernando Torres, Carragher's bit on the side!

## LOCAL-OU-HERO

As many fans coined their own 'Torres'-style chants, a couple stood out for their originality – if a copy can claim any originality. When Chelsea played Liverpool in the 2008 Champions League semi-final, they were heading for a first-leg defeat until John Arne Riise managed to head Salomon Kalou's cross into his own net in stoppage time. Chelsea went on to reach the final after a second-leg extra-time win and the following song could soon be heard from the Stamford Bridge diehards:

He comes from the Ivory Coast,
Kalou, Kalou,
He don't do coke like Adrian
Mutu, Mutu,
He crossed the ball from the left,
It landed right on Riise's head,
That's why we love Salomon Kalou!

## ENOCH'S BIG MOMENT

Leeds United's Nigerian striker Enoch Showunmi was the subject of another 'Torres'-style chant with his fans composing this bizarre effort. Showunmi was rumoured to be rather well endowed – dressing room gossip tends to travel fast.

Despite the fact he was never more than a bit-part player during his time at Elland Road – his squad number of 21 tells its own story – the chant that was created for him ensured he'd be a cult hero forever in Yorkshire. In fact, the song followed him around and was subsequently sung by Falkirk fans (with an amended ending):

> Enoch has got a massive cock,
> Enoch, Enoch,
> Enoch has got a massive cock
> Enoch, Enoch,
> He shagged a woman, now she's dead,
> He swings his cock around his head,
> Enoch Showunmi, United's 21!

## STEVIE G FORCE

Liverpool also created another popular chant for one of their heroes, with Steven Gerrard the recipient this time. The all-action Liverpool-born midfielder is a hero to thousands on Merseyside and The Kop saluted him by singing the following song to the tune of 'Que Sera, Sera':

> Steve Gerrard, Gerrard,
> He'll pass the ball 40 yards,
> He's big and he's fucking hard,
> Steve Gerrard, Gerrard

Gerrard applauded the choice of music on the Anfield PA system.

## ▦ STEVIE G FLEE

Gerrard's loyalty to Liverpool came under severe pressure when he was courted by Chelsea twice in 2004 and 2006. With the newspapers full of rumours of the Londoners swooping for Liverpool's star man, there was even talk of the England midfielder having handed in a transfer request.

Whatever did happen and however close he came to leaving, his final decision was to stay at Anfield, but that didn't stop Man United fans crowing (Chelsea and Arsenal fans also sang this) when the clubs met later in 2006. And, to really rub it in, they used Liverpool's Gerrard song to make their point:

> Steve Gerrard, Gerrard,
> He kisses the badge on his chest,
> Then puts in a transfer request,
> Steve Gerrard, Gerrard!

## ▦ TOM'S APPETITE FOR SUCCESS

Arsenal fans were suitably impressed with the early performances of their new centre-back Thomas Vermaelen when he joined the club in 2009. The Belgian showed huge promise after signing from Ajax for £10 million, to the extent that the Gunners fans thought the Premier League's established strikers would struggle against their star man. Surprisingly enough, they managed to present these sentiments in the form of this eloquent song to the tune of 'Oh My Darling, Clementine':

> Tom Vermaelen,
> Tom Vermaelen,
> Tom Vermaelen number Five,
> Fuck your Rooneys,
> Fuck your Drogbas,
> 'Cos he'll eat those c*nts alive!

## ▦ INSIDE JOB

Ask Middlesbrough fans to name their most famous recent players and names like Juninho and Ravanelli will probably come up fairly often – but so will

Joseph-Desire Job. The Cameroon midfielder was a decent enough performer at the Riverside, but his impact was certainly not felt like some other famous sons of the club. Yet he'll always have a special place in the hearts of Boro fans as a result of the cult chant that was sung in his honour, which played on his name and reflected the economic hardships of life in the area.

To the tune of 'Guantanamera', Boro fans chanted:

> One Job on Teesside,
> There's only one Job on Teesside!

## ▦ PAYING TRIBUTE TO ANDERSON

Highly rated Brazilian midfielder Anderson is also a cult figure at Old Trafford, but probably not because of his inconsistent displays for Man United. Some of Anderson's off-pitch antics – including allegedly being part of a sex party with prostitutes alongside teammates Cristiano Ronaldo and Nani – had earned him respect on the terraces. This also earned him a highly catchy chant, sung to the tune of Black Lace classic 'Agadoo':

> Anderson-son-son,
> He's better than Kleberson,
> Anderson-son-son,
> He's our midfield magician,
> To the left, to the right,
> To the samba beat all night,
> He is class with a brass,
> And he shits on Fabregas!

## ▦ NOVAK CLEANS UP

Hitting the headlines before you've made your first-team debut is an excellent way to make sure your new fans notice you. Huddersfield's young striker Lee Novak 'tangled' with Newcastle's Fabricio Coloccini according to post-match reports from a bad-tempered pre-season friendly between the clubs. Soon after, he was making the right kind of news by scoring 14 goals in his first season for the club.

Sharp-witted Terriers fans quickly came up with an unforgettable anthem for their young forward, to the tune of 'Sloop John B':

> We've got Novak,
> We've got Novak,
> Our carpets are filthy,
> We've got Novak!

## ⊞ KANU ROLLS BACK THE YEARS

When they're not belting out the 'Pompey Chimes', Portsmouth fans still have time to laud their heroes, specifically Nigerian striker Kanu.

The description 'evergreen' is used to describe players who still seem to be able to make an impact despite being, er, old. Kanu's real age, like many of his Nigerian counterparts, has been the subject of much debate since he came to play in the Premier League for Arsenal. This follows a two-year ban from all international competition imposed on Nigeria by FIFA, after it was discovered that players who played for them in the 1988 Olympics had given different dates of birth from previous competitions in which they had taken part.

Nigerian bloggers have speculated that Kanu, aged 33 in 2010, was really 42 by that stage; and so Pompey composed this chant for their striker, to the tune of 'Que Sera, Sera':

> King Kanu, Kanu,
> He's older than me and you,
> His real age is 62,
> King Kanu, Kanu

## ⊞ WALK IN THE PARK

Xenophobia, racism or good-natured banter? The jury's still out, and probably will be forever, but judge for yourselves from this selection of songs about South Korean Premier League players.

Man United's Ji-Sung Park is much loved at Old Trafford as much for his all-energy midfield displays as for the song that fans sing about him. Without a doubt one of the most original to have emerged from United in

City's Nigel de Jong had taken the instruction to 'follow Park's every move' a little too seriously.

years, the Park song even finds time to insult Liverpudlians as well as Koreans, probably.

This is sung to the tune of 'Lord of the Dance':

> Park, Park, wherever you may be,
> You eat dogs in your own country,
> But it could be worse,
> You could be Scouse,
> Eating rats in your council house!

## ▦ PARK'S BITE TO EAT

They might have left it there, but a new chant emerged purely concentrating on the unusual South Korean delicacy of dog. This time, United fans went back to basics with this song to the tune of 'Ten Green Bottles', with the possibility of continuing all the way down to zero:

There were ten Alsatians walking down the street,
Ten Alsatians walking down the street,
But if Ji-Sung Park should fancy one to eat…
There'd be nine Alsatians walking down the street!

## ▦ READING GO DOGGING

Fortunately, there weren't that many South Korean footballers playing in the Premier League at the time or there may have been a dog-eating chant epidemic. However, Reading fans also managed to force their way into the act, with a song about Seol Ki-Hyeon, along very similar lines:

He'll shoot,
He'll score,
He'll eat your labrador,
Seol Ki-Hyeon, Seol Ki-Hyeon!

## ▦ THE FRUITS OF LEE'S LABOUR

Perhaps the greatest hero – or victim – of chanting has to be former Nottingham Forest striker Jason Lee. The forward sported a distinctive hairstyle by tying up his dreadlocks so that they stood on top of his head, giving him a not too dissimilar appearance to a pineapple.

The journeyman striker would probably have remained as obscure as any other footballer who played for a long list of teams, had it not been for his shooting to fame on TV's *Fantasy Football*, where Frank Skinner and David Baddiel ridiculed his haircut and his inability to score goals for Nottingham Forest (although he did score 14 goals in 76 appearances for them).

The striker's hair and poor form saw him become a near-weekly fixture for lampooning by the two comedians and led not only to the following chant being sung by opposition fans, as encouraged by Skinner and Baddiel to the tune of 'The Whole World in his Hands', but also to the shaving of Lee's head:

He's got a pineapple on his head,
He's got a pineapple on his head!

## ▦ QUINN STRUTS HIS STUFF

It's hard to imagine Sunderland chairman Niall Quinn in a pair of disco pants, but Man City fans made sure his cult status was preserved forever with their early nineties classic. The fans warmed immediately to the big Irish striker, following his signing from Arsenal in 1990, and his 66 goals and tireless effort over the next six years helped cement his reputation.

The icing on the cake was provided during a league match against Derby in 1991 when Quinn managed the (probably) unique feat of scoring early on and then saving a penalty to help his side to a 2-1 win. With no reserve goalkeeper on the bench in those days, Quinn was forced to don the goalie gloves after Tony Coton had been sent off and stopped the resulting Dean Saunders spot-kick.

This is the chant City fans sang to the tune of 'Stars and Stripes Forever':

> Niall Quinn's disco pants are the best,
> They go up from his arse to his chest,
> They are better than Adam & The Ants,
> Niall Quinn's disco pants!"

## ▦ JIMMY THE KING

Jimmy Bullard has been a hero to many sets of fans, such is his personality and love of the lighter side of the game.

While at Fulham, he suffered a serious knee injury that kept him out of football for more than a year but he returned at around the same time that Roy Hodgson was appointed manager. Together, the pair helped to resurrect the team's fortunes as they had seemed to be heading for relegation until that point.

But a tremendous end to the season, in which the club took 12 points from their last five games, saw them to safety and Bullard's midfield prowess was celebrated with this chant to the tune of 'Que Sera, Sera':

> Jim Bullard, Bullard
> He's better than Steve Gerrard,
> He's thinner than Frank Lampard,
> Jim Bullard, Bullard

# ▥ DOING THE AMEOBI

While Shola Ameobi may not go down in history as one of the Premier League's great strikers, his impact on Newcastle's Gallowgate End will always be immense. The Toon Army had a moment of inspiration when they came up with their tribute to one of their favourite, if slightly maligned, sons with this chant, complete with actions, to the tune of kids favourite the 'Hokey Cokey':

Shola loved the part where you had to 'put your whole self in'.

You put your left foot in,
Your left foot out,
In out, in out, you shake it all about,
You do the Ameobi and you turn around,
That's what it's all about.
Woah! Shola Ameobi,
Woah! Shola Ameobi,
Woah! Shola Ameobi,
Knees bend, arms stretched
Ra! Ra! Ra!

# YORKE'S VILLA SCORE

Dwight Yorke is another of football's fun-loving players and his laid-back approach to life, coupled with his eye for goal, means he's been loved wherever he's played.

At Aston Villa, the Holte End were particularly fond of the Trinidad and Tobago international, who was known as 'The Smiling Assassin' – he usually hit the target and he always had a grin on his face. Well, you *did* ask.

He was discovered playing in the West Indies by then Villa manager Graham Taylor who brought him over to Birmingham and 73 goals in 232 appearances repaid that faith. The Villa fans cleverly played on his name to sing this novel chant to the tune of 'New York, New York':

> Start spreading the news,
> He's playing today,
> I want to see him score again,
> Dwight Yorke, Dwight Yorke
> If he can score from there,
> He'll score from, anywhere,
> It's up to you Dwight Yorke, Dwight Yorke!

# FOLICALLY CHALLENGED FEENEY

Journeyman pro Warren Feeney wouldn't be first in many fans' lists of their favourite players, but the striker has won the hearts of his hometown fans. The former Bournemouth, Stockport, Luton and Cardiff forward always performed consistently in the Football League but it was at international level where his hero worship occurred.

The Belfast-born Northern Ireland international became something of a cult figure when turning out for his country, particularly due to his prominent shaved and shiny head – although at 5ft 10in, he was by no means a small footballer. Either way, his countrymen sang the following song, whose tune will need no explanation:

> We love our itsy-bitsy, teeny-weeny,
> Baldy headed Warren Feeney!

## KEANE'S LIMI-TED ANFIELD SPELL

Robbie Keane's trip to Merseyside was more short-lived than he would have imagined, but he did manage to leave a lasting impression. The Spurs striker joined the Anfield club in the summer of 2008 but he was back in north London by the end of the following January transfer window.

He scored five goals in 19 appearances for the club, but it will be the chant the Kop sang for him, celebrating his broad Irish accent, to the tune of 'Quartermaster's Store', that will be remembered far more than his football:

He's fast, he's red,
He talks like Father Ted,
Robbie Keane, Robbie Keane!

## VOICE OF AN ANGEL

Fans of wordplay will be thrilled at the song Aston Villa fans came up with for Colombian striker Juan Pablo Angel. Indeed, there must be some wordsmiths in the Holte End for this bilingual treat to have made itself heard loud and proud. For, quite simply, the Villa fans sang the following to the tune of 'Guantanamera':

Juan Pablo Angel,
There's only Juan Pablo Angel!

## WISE WORDS

Many Millwall fans would argue their reputation for hooliganism is unfair, and they're right. But some of their songs don't do them any favours. In 2004, when Dennis Wise led the Lions on an incredible run to the FA Cup final, the fans concocted a deliciously wicked chant for their leader. Using Arsenal's 'Volare' for inspiration the Millwall masses sang:

Oh Wisey, woah-oh, oh Wisey, woah-oh,
He's only 5 foot 4,
He'll break your fucking jaw!

# ALVIN MARTIN

**Alvin Martin was Mr West Ham.** Over a period of 19 years, the central defender played 469 games for the East End club, giving his all in every single one of them. And how did those fans repay him? With a chant that he despised. 'The West Ham fans used to sing "He's got no hair, but we don't care... Alvin Martin!" (to the tune of "Hooray, Hooray, It's a Holi-Holiday"),' he says.

'That became associated with me and people remember me for that song, but why couldn't they have come up with something better than that?

'To be fair, the fans also used to chant "Alvin, sort him out! Alvin, Alvin, sort him out" whenever there was any trouble on the pitch.'

But, when it comes to nominating his favourite, the Bootle-born former England international picks one much closer to home. 'If you said to me "is there a song that sticks out in your mind above all others that's connected to football" it would be "You'll Never Walk Alone". Even now when I go to football – and I'm biased because I was a Liverpool supporter – on the right night, it can make the hairs on the back of your neck stand up.'

Alvin Martin always 'encouraged' his opponents to have a sit-down during a game.

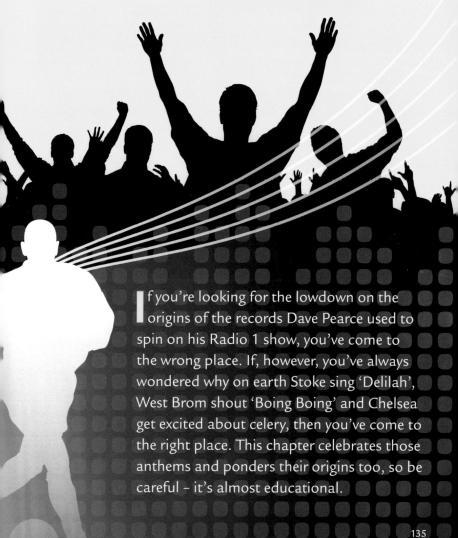

# 10

# CLUB ANTHEMS

I f you're looking for the lowdown on the origins of the records Dave Pearce used to spin on his Radio 1 show, you've come to the wrong place. If, however, you've always wondered why on earth Stoke sing 'Delilah', West Brom shout 'Boing Boing' and Chelsea get excited about celery, then you've come to the right place. This chapter celebrates those anthems and ponders their origins too, so be careful – it's almost educational.

# ▦ STOKE GO POTTY FOR DELILAH

Mention Stoke City to any football fan and almost immediately they'll utter the name 'Delilah' – as much as Liverpool are known for 'You'll Never Walk Alone', the Potters have become synonymous with the Tom Jones hit.

Stoke fans started singing the song in the eighties. Legend has it that after an away match at Derby, several fans were enjoying a few drinks and a singsong in a pub when police intervened and asked them

Tom Jones, seconds after receiving a fresh batch of ladies' undies in the post.

not to chant anything with swear words. At almost the same time, 'Delilah' started playing on the jukebox, the fans joined in and it quickly caught on.

One of the fans in that pub was Anton Booth, whose nickname TJ is the original artist's initials, and he is always given the honour of starting the song, usually from the vantage point of someone's shoulders, or while being hoisted high in the air. His fellow fans sing his nickname until silence falls and he sings the opening lines, only assisted by other Stoke supporters at the end of each line until he utters 'she stood there laughing' at which point everyone else joins in.

The original lyrics have been slightly twisted over the years and it's now commonplace for Stoke fans to replace the line 'I felt the knife in my hand' with 'I put my dick in her hand' – whether Mr Jones would approve is unknown.

Here, in all its glory, is the version Stoke currently sing:

At break of day when that man drove away, I was waiting (woah-oh!),
I cross the street to her house and she opened the door (woah-oh!),
She stood there laughing (Ha! Ha! Ha! Ha!),
I put my dick in her hand and she laughed no more.
Why, why, why Delilah?
Why, why, why Delilah?
So before you come to break down the door,
Forgive me Delilah I just couldn't take any more.
Why, why, why Delilah?

## ⦚ MAN CITY FANS MOON

Like 'Delilah', 'Blue Moon' has now become the official anthem of Manchester City fans although it's not widely known that the song was first adopted by fans of Crewe Alexandra. In the eighties, Alex fans would serenade their beloved at Gresty Road with the song and it wasn't until the first day of the 1989/90 season that Man City fans first used it. And even then, this was at the end of a game against Liverpool at Anfield, long after the teams had left the pitch, and was more of an afterthought than anything else.

But it caught on and as the season went on, there was no City game that didn't feature the song being chanted at least once. Nowadays, City fans still sing it religiously and tend to cover the first verse:

> Blue Moon,
> You saw me standing alone,
> Without a dream in my heart,
> Without a love of my own

## ⦚ CHELSEA'S LOVE AFFAIR WITH CELERY

Why have one club anthem when you can have two? For the last three decades two songs have dominated the repertoire of all Chelsea fans and they both share the same level of unlikelihood. As club legend has it, both songs emerged out of the glamour of a 1981 pre-season tour of Sweden (in stark contrast to the club's usual tour of the USA in these Roman Abramovich-funded years). A small group of fans, including the legendary Micky Greenaway, followed the Blues out to Scandinavia armed with, among other things, a cassette which contained a Chas & Dave number called 'Ask Old Brown'. The lyrics of this song went:

> Ask Old Brown to tea,
> And his family,
> If he don't come
> I'll tickle his bum with a lump of celery

Clearly, one or two tipples would've been consumed by the fans and Greenaway is said to have repeatedly played the track and, before long, a new Chelsea anthem had been born as the fans chanted to the tune of 'Wem-ber-lee':

Celery, Celery,
If she don't come
I'll tickle her bum with a lump of celery!

And along with the song came a trend of bringing the named vegetable to matches to throw onto the pitch. This remained popular for many years until the club were forced to ban celery from Stamford Bridge in 2007. This followed various incidents at the League Cup final between Chelsea and Arsenal, during which Gunners players had been bombarded with the vegetable when they went to take corners. Chelsea were then forced to make the following statement:

'The throwing of anything at a football match, including celery, is a criminal offence for which you can be arrested and end up with a criminal record. In future, if anyone is found attempting to bring celery into Stamford Bridge they could be refused entry and anyone caught throwing celery will face a ban.'

## ▦ CHELSEA SING IN NUMBERS

When they're not chanting about vegetables, Blues fans will invariably be brushing up on their favourite kids' tunes instead – especially one designed to improve their counting skills. The Sweden tour was not just home to a Chas & Dave tape, it also featured a cassette full of children's favourites including 'One Man Went to Mow' – and 'King of the Shed End' Greenaway was at it again with several plays of the tune. Following the tour, some fans continued to sing 'One Man Went to Mow' in various pubs before matches and, before long, it became a Stamford Bridge staple and is still chanted everywhere Chelsea go today:

One man went to mow (mow!)
Went to mow a meadow,
One man and his dog – Spot!
Went to mow a meadow
Two men went to mow (mow!)
Went to mow a meadow,
Two men, one man and his dog – Spot!
Went to mow a meadow

And so on until after ten men, when the chant ends with:

Chelsea (clap, clap, clap)
Chelsea (clap, clap, clap)
Chelsea (clap, clap, clap)

## LIVERPOOL HOLD THEIR HEADS UP HIGH

When the words to a song are displayed for all to see on the entrance gates of your club, it's a pretty safe bet that's one powerful anthem you have. When you're welcomed through Anfield's Shankly Gates, 'You'll Never Walk Alone' greets you at the door.

Originally composed by Rogers and Hammerstein for the musical *Carousel*, the song became popular when Merseybeat group Gerry and the Pacemakers released it as a single in 1963. It became synonymous with the club soon after its release just at the time when singing in football stadiums was really taking off. The story goes that Gerry Marsden himself passed a recording of the song on to Liverpool manager Bill Shankly in 1963, who was highly impressed with its motivational themes.

The game was off unless somebody from the council would come and unlock the gates.

The song became so popular as an inspirational anthem that it was also adopted by Celtic and many other European clubs, but will forever be the Anfield side's official anthem, played before the beginning of every match. These are the opening verses and chorus:

When you walk through a storm,
Hold your head up high,
And don't be afraid of the dark
At the end of the storm,
Is a golden sky,
And the sweet silver song of the lark
Walk on through the wind,
Walk on through the rain,
Though your dreams be tossed and blown
Walk on, walk on, with hope in your heart,
And you'll never walk alone,
You'll never walk alone

## WEST BROM'S SONGS OF PRAISE

The effect of Liverpool's 'You'll Never Walk Alone' was felt across British football, as many supporters wanted their own clubs to adopt an anthem.

Many people incorrectly assume that West Brom's famous 'Boing Boing' chant is their anthem, but in fact the Hawthorns has rung out to the unlikely tune of 'The Lord is My Shepherd' since the mid-seventies. Taken from Psalm 23 and sung to the tune of the hymn, there is little obvious connection to the Black Country club, but an anthem was wanted, and an anthem they got.

Since the 1992/93 season, when the club were stuck in English football's third tier, Albion fans began celebrating goals with their famous 'Boing Boing Baggies' chant, which involved jumping up and down while saying those very words. This still remains a firm favourite, but there is only one Baggies anthem:

The Lord's my Shepherd, I'll not want,
He makes me down to lie.
In pastures green he leadeth me
The quiet waters by

Repeat first verse then:

The West Brom (clap, clap, clap) – repeat three more times

## ▦ GEORDIES' RACY FOLK SONG

One of the oldest songs still chanted on the terraces today is the Newcastle United anthem 'Blaydon Races'. It's a song rich in local history and tradition, but like the best anthems, it doesn't directly reference the football club.

Written by appropriately named folk singer Geordie Ridley in 1862, the song celebrates the popular race meeting and fair held at Blaydon, a Gateshead town, and charts the four-mile journey from Newcastle to the racecourse venue.

Many other versions of the song have been sung with fans replacing key words to suit their own teams (Man United have a version about 'Matt Busby's aces') but this is the original, with the following opening lyrics appearing in pure Geordie (with no subtitles):

Aw went to Blaydon Races, 'twas on the ninth of Joon,
Eiteen hundred an' sixty-two, on a summer's efternoon,
Aw tyuk the 'bus frae Balmbra's, an' she wis heavy laden,
Away we went alang Collingwood Street, that's on the road to Blaydon.
Ah me lads, ye shud only seen us gannin',
We pass'd the foaks upon the road just as they wor stannin',
Thor wes lots o' lads an' lasses there, all wi' smiling faces,
Gawn alang the Scotswood Road, to see the Blaydon Races

## ▦ PALACE FEELING GLAD ALL OVER

Shortly after Liverpool fans converted 'You'll Never Walk Alone' from a pub sing-along to terrace anthem, Crystal Palace fans managed the same feat with 'Glad All Over'. The Dave Clark Five had a hit with the song in 1964 and, although the band hailed from north London, the south London side adopted the song as an anthem as fans sang along to it before, during and after matches.

In 1990, when the Eagles reached the FA Cup final, the squad recorded a (far more inferior) version of the song, as per the tradition at the time. These days, Palace fans tend to sing the following verse and chorus – accompanied by a loud PA system at Selhurst Park:

You say that you love me (say you love me!),
All of the time (all of the time!).

You say that you need me (say you need me!),
You'll always be mine (always be mine!).
And I'm feeling (clap clap)
Glad all over,
Yes I'm (clap clap)
Glad all over,
Baby I'm (clap clap)
Glad all over,
So glad you're mine

## ▦ LEEDS MARCH TOGETHER

Leeds United's 'Marching on Together' (or 'Leeds! Leeds! Leeds!' to give it its official title) is a good example of an anthem which was written specifically for the football club. Originally the B-side to United's 1972 FA Cup final song 'Leeds United', the track quickly became a firm favourite at Elland Road and is always played before kick-off, with supporters standing and saluting their players. Fans also sing the chorus throughout matches and 'Marching on Together' has become the closest thing possible to an official club motto without actually being one. These are the opening verses and chorus:

Here we go with Leeds United,
We're gonna give the boys a hand,
Stand up and sing for Leeds United,
They are the greatest in the land.
(na na na)
Everyday, we're all gonna say,
We love you Leeds! Leeds! Leeds!
Everywhere, we're gonna be there,
We love you Leeds! Leeds! Leeds!
Marching on together!
We're gonna see you win,
(na na na na na na)
We are so proud,
We shout it out loud,
We love you Leeds! Leeds! Leeds!

# ▓ THE HAMMERS BUBBLE OVER

'I'm Forever Blowing Bubbles' is the official anthem of West Ham, whose fans always sing the chorus of the old music hall number during matches. Of that there is no debate. Of the song's connection to the club, there is, however, much debate with theories and counter-theories abounding.

The song became popular in music halls during the 1920s and was one of many played by the Beckton Gas Works Band at Upton Park before matches. It seems likely that Hammers fans would have sung along and the rest is history. However, some football historians have dug up evidence of Swansea City fans singing the song during an FA Cup tie against West Ham, making that the point from which it became an Upton Park hit. And on top of that, there's the theory that youth team player Will Murray's curly hair resembled the child's in an advert for Pears Soap's Bubbles, earning him the nickname Bubbles Murray – and a chant in his honour.

So, take all those stories, throw in another about real East Enders singing the song in air raid shelters during the Blitz, and take your pick. What is

Bow-ties were de rigueur on the terraces in the East End.

certain is that Hammers fans have slightly altered some of the words and this is the version they currently sing home and away:

> I'm forever blowing bubbles,
> Pretty bubbles in the air.
> They fly so high,
> They reach the sky,
> And like my dreams,
> They fade and die.
> Fortune's always hiding,
> I've looked everywhere,
> I'm forever blowing bubbles,
> Pretty bubbles in the air.
> United! (clap clap clap)
> United! (clap clap clap)

## ▦ BLADES GO FOR A BUTTY

It's difficult to imagine what John Denver would make of it, but Sheffield United's 'Greasy Chip Butty' remains one of the most original and inspiring anthems sung on the terraces. Based on Denver's beautifully melodic 'Annie's Song', Blades fans arrived with their own version during the mid-eighties, which celebrated all of the city's local delights. And it fast became an unofficial club anthem which has been widely imitated by other clubs, who swap the Sheffield references to suit their own local delicacies.

Early versions of the song had the last line 'I just can't get enough' to rhyme with the snuff line, but this was soon adapted to stick closer to Denver's original:

> You fill up my senses
> Like a gallon of Magnet,
> Like a packet of Woodbines,
> Like a good pinch of snuff,
> Like a night out in Sheffield,
> Like a greasy chip butty,
> Like Sheffield United, Come fill me again!
> na na na na na naaaaa, oooh!

# ▦ THE END OF THE BIRMINGHAM ROAD

Another highly original anthem is Birmingham City's 'Keep Right On', a song that was actually born out of Scotland during the First World War. The original version was composed and performed by Sir Harry Lauder, who channelled his grief at the news of his son's death on the battlefields to write a moving tribute song. Inspired by stories that his son had instructed his fellow troops to 'Carry on' despite his imminent demise, Lauder came up with 'Keep Right on to the End of the Road', which became a hugely popular Scottish song following the war.

It wasn't until 1956 and the Blues' run to the FA Cup final that the song was adopted by their fans via the voice of their popular Scottish winger Alex Govan, who sung it on the team bus on the way to Leyton Orient for a fourth round match.

The song caught on among the squad and when they made the trip to play Arsenal in the quarter-finals, Govan and his teammates bellowed it out on the way to the ground and through the open windows to the gathered Birmingham fans when they arrived at Highbury. The fans loved it, sung it themselves and it stood the test of time.

Over the years, the first verse has been adapted from the original to lend it more of an association with the Midlands club and this is the version Blues fans now sing:

As you go through life it's a long, long road,
There'll be joys and sorrows too.
As we journey on we will sing this song
For the boys in royal blue.
We're often partisan (clap clap clap)
We will journey on (clap clap clap)
Keep right on to the end of the road,
Keep right on to the end.
Though the way be long let your heart beat strong,
Keep right on to the end.
Though you're tired and weary,
Still journey on 'til you come to your happy abode.
With all our love we'll be dreaming of,
We'll be there. Where? At the end of the road.
Birmingham (clap clap clap) Birmingham (clap clap clap)

## ▦ FOXES KEEP SMILING

In what must be the only example of a football club anthem being started by an old dear with absolutely no interest in the team, Leicester City sing the Louis Armstrong hit 'When You're Smiling'. Back in 1967, young Leicester fans used to drink in the Three Cranes pub on a Saturday night alongside plenty of domino-playing old women. Without fail, and aided by ale, some of these women would break into song towards the end of the evening and one of these melodies would be 'When You're Smiling'.

Although the song was completely unknown to the more junior fans, it quickly caught on and with buses for away games picking up fans from the Three Cranes, it wasn't long before songs from the pub were chanted on the bus – especially the Armstrong track. The bus song quickly became a terrace anthem and has remained that way ever since, although Foxes fans tend to sing it a great deal faster than Armstrong ever did:

When you're smiling,
When you're smiling,
The whole world smiles with you.

When you're laughing,
When you're laughing,
The sun comes shining through.

But when you're crying,
You bring on the rain,
So stop your sighing,
Be happy again.
Keep on smiling,
Cause when you're smiling,
The whole world smiles with you,
The whole world smiles with you,
The whole world smiles with you,
The Leicester! (clap clap clap)
The Leicester! (clap clap clap)

## ▦ AND IT'S GOODNIGHT FROM ROVERS

If the thought of Leicester fans singing Louis Armstrong is odd, thousands of Bristol Rovers supporters chanting American folk song 'Goodnight Irene', with its themes of love and suicide, is even weirder.

Leadbelly often fell asleep mid-verse.

Originally performed and written by Leadbelly but covered many times, the song was adopted by Rovers fans as early as 1951 – it's thought that during a match between Rovers and Plymouth Argyle, the Plymouth fans had sung 'Goodnight Irene' to taunt Rovers fans as their team led 1-0, only for Rovers to turn the match on its head and win 3-1. The victory was celebrated by Rovers fans who chanted 'Goodnight Argyle' back to Plymouth to the tune of 'Goodnight Irene'.

Soon after, the original song was heard at many Rovers games and is just as popular 60 years later:

> Irene, goodnight Irene,
> Irene Goodnight,
> Goodnight Irene, Goodnight Irene,
> I'll see you in my dreams!

## ▦ NORWICH STAY ON THE BALL

Lauded as the world's oldest football song still being sung today, Norwich City's anthem dates back to the 19th century. Its precise origins are unknown but it is believed to have been penned for local teams in the Norfolk area like Norwich Teachers, Swifans or CEYMS, all of whom played long before the formation of the Canaries in 1902.

The lyrics sound as dated as a Victorian football song should, but the Norwich fans still sing this part of the chant before all their home games:

Kick it off, throw it in, have a little scrimmage,
Keep it low, a splendid rush, bravo, win or die.
On the ball, City, never mind the danger,
Steady on, now's your chance,
Hurrah! We've scored a goal.
City! [clap clap clap]
City! [clap clap clap]
City! [clap clap clap]"

## ▦ POMPEY RING OUT A CLASSIC

Another club laying claim to still singing the oldest ever football chant is Portsmouth for their 'Pompey Chimes' – although today's song is different from the original in terms of the tune and the words.

Ironically, it was not the Navy that first brought the song to Portsmouth but the Army, as the Royal Artillery was the town's team in the 1890s. They played at a ground close to the Guildhall clock, which would chime every 15 minutes so referees would use it to know when to blow for half-time and full-time. The fans would also join in by reminding the referee to blow as the clock ticked towards the hour mark.

When the Royal Artillery were expelled from the FA Amateur Cup for allegations of professionalism, the team fell into decline and many of their fans transferred allegiances to Portsmouth, taking the chant with them.

The official handbook of Portsmouth FC for 1900 states these are the words to the 'Pompey Chimes':

Play up Pompey,
Just one more goal,
Make tracks, What ho!
Hallo! Hallo!'

It's probably just as well that Portsmouth fans today sing a far more simple – and less embarrassing version which is simply:

Play up Pompey,
Pompey play up!

# BLUEBIRDS WILL BE THERE

A third chant still sung today which has been heard on the terraces for the best part of a hundred years is Cardiff's distinctive 'I'll be There'. It was first heard in 1926 at the time of the General Strike and was a song that linked the mining communities of South Wales. The song is very much woven into the fabric of the club. And given its very specific mining references, it's not one that would ever be lifted by fans of rival teams.

These days, when they're not jumping up and down doing the Ayatollah, Cardiff fans usually just sing the chorus, however, this is the original first verse along with the singalong part:

> When the coal comes from the Rhondda,
> And the water's running fine,
> With my little pick and shovel,
> I'll be there.
> I'll be there, I'll be there,
> With my little pick and shovel,
> I'll be there

# BRISTOL'S CIDER SONG RULES

Whereas Cardiff fans are brought together by coal, Bristol City fans have drinking as the focal point of their cultural heritage. They are also fortunate (or unfortunate, depending on your viewpoint) to have local band The Wurzels to compose several songs in celebration of their favourite tipple, cider. One song, 'I am a Cider Drinker' has been adopted by the East End section of Ashton Gate, but the club anthem and fans' favourite is 'Drink Up Thy Zider'.

The original lyrics of the chorus have been altered to reflect the rivalry with Bristol Rovers and City fans tend to just repeat the chorus as follows:

> Drink up thee cider,
> Drink up thee cider,
> For tonight we'll merry be (merry be).
> We'll go on down to Rovers,
> To do the bastards over,
> And still pour cider in thee jar

## ▦ GRIMSBY'S FISHY CHANT

So, Cardiff have coal, Bristol City have cider and Grimsby Town have... fish.

The Mariners are not so-called for nothing and the local trade is reflected in fans' anthem 'Sing When We're Fishing' which simply replaces the word 'winning' from the popular chant 'Sing When You're Winning' to the tune of 'Guantanamera':

> Sing when we're fishing,
> We only sing when we're fishing,
> Sing when we're fishing,
> We only sing when we're fishing

And just in case you're on an away trip to the fishing port or visiting for any other reason and fancy some local fare, the Town fans also like to taunt away fans by chanting:

> We piss on your fish,
> Yes we do, yes we do!

## ▦ FOREST LOVE THAT FEELING

Nottingham Forest can boast that they're probably the only club who have an anthem which exists solely to taunt their opponents. And not just their rivals, but any team they happen to be playing. Whenever Forest take the lead, once their fans have finished celebrating they immediately turn to the opposition fans, point their fingers and sing:

> You've lost that loving feeling,
> Woah-oh, that loving feeling,
> You've lost that loving feeling,
> Now it's gone, gone, gone, woah-oh-woah-oh-woah!

Forest fans also have a competing anthem in which they eulogise their City Ground home, using the tune of 'Mull of Kintyre':

City Ground,
Oh mist rolling in from the Trent.
My desire,
Is always to be here,
Oh City Ground

## ▦ CHARLTON'S VALLEY OF LIFE

And Forest aren't the only club to use that tune. Charlton Athletic fans have had plenty of ups and downs, especially when they went homeless for more than seven years between 1985 and 1992. And that's exactly why The Valley has retained huge significance to the club and is the basis for the fans' anthem 'Valley Floyd Road', an original song, which is also chanted to 'Mull of Kintyre' (the Floyd Road in question is the club's address):

Many miles have I travelled,
Many games have I seen,
Following Charlton my favourite team,
Many hours have I spent in the Covered End Choir,
Singing Valley Floyd Road,
My only desire,
Valley Floyd Road,
The mist rolling in from the Thames, my desire,
Is always to be found at Valley Floyd Road

## ▦ THE SUN SHINES ON HIBERNIAN

Arguably the most stirring club anthem is Hibernian's 'Sunshine on Leith', a song written and performed by Hibs fans The Proclaimers. Although the song, which is also the title of a Proclaimers album, is not necessarily sung every week by the Easter Road fans, it's saved for special occasions, which only adds to the fervour with which it's sung and the emotion it creates.

The song is written by people from the north Edinburgh town of Leith for the people of Leith, which is where the club is based, and these are the lyrics:

One of The Proclaimers was determined to stick to his vow of silence.

My heart was broken, my heart was broken,
Sorrow, sorrow, sorrow, sorrow,
My heart was broken, my heart was broken,
You saw it, you claimed it, you touched it, you saved it,
My tears are drying, my tears are drying,
Thank you, thank you, thank you, thank you,
My tears are drying, my tears are drying,
Your beauty and kindness made tears clear my blindness,
While I'm worth my room on this Earth, I will be with you,
While the chief puts sunshine on Leith, I'll thank him for his work,
And your birth and my birth, yeah, yeah, yeah, yeah, yeah...

## JUST LIKE WATCHING BARNSLEY

Barnsley famously enjoyed a season in the Premier League spotlight back in 1997 and their fans found a song to go with their exploits. Although plenty of copycat versions have since been aired, the Tykes were the first to serenade their fans by singing this, to the tune of 'Blue Moon':

Brazil!
It's just like watching Brazil,
It's just like watching Brazil,
It's just like watching Brazil

Although they only lasted a season in the top flight, the song will always be linked with that campaign and the club even tried to get in on the act when they launched a yellow 'Brazil' away strip for the 2001/02 season. Unfortunately, Barnsley were relegated to the third tier of English football that year.

## GILLINGHAM DO THE WALTZ

As the only professional club in Kent, Gillingham have every right to a special anthem and they haven't disappointed. Engelbert Humperdinck's 'The Last Waltz' doesn't spring to mind as the most obvious terrace hit, but the Gills managed to find a way to make it work. The song was first sung by fans at the end of the 1973/74 season when it was played at Peterborough's London Road, when both clubs were celebrating promotion to the old Third Division.

The song continued to be heard for a few years after that but then went out of fashion only to make a comeback when the Gills enjoyed a spell in the Championship at the turn of the century and it's still sung today.

Fans at the Priestfield Stadium's Rainham End have altered Humperdinck's original line 'Just my tears and the orchestra singing' which then leads into a 'la la la' interlude, to something more suitable, followed by a switch to a 'Hey Jude' finale:

I had the last waltz with you,
Two lonely people together.
I fell in love with you,
The last waltz should last forever.
It's all over now,
Nothing else to say,
Just the Gills and the Rainham End singing:
La, la, la, la, la la, la,
La la la la,
The Gills!

## ⦚ POSH THEY ARE

Despite Gillingham's nicking, sorry, adopting of 'The Last Waltz', it still remains a Peterborough United anthem, but seeing as we've just heard about it, let's focus on the other Posh anthem.

'Posh We Are' is a song written specially for the London Road club by Brian Paine and Tony Pickering back in the seventies, and was then re-recorded in 2008 by The Lightyears to celebrate the club's impending promotion to the Championship.

Here's part of it as it's far too long:

> Peterborough, Peterborough, Peterborough la la la,
> Peterborough, Peterborough, Peterborough la la la.
> We're singing along with the feeling,
> We're gonna conquer the league,
> Now we're at the double,
> So look out for trouble,
> And all you others take heed.
> It's Posh we are and Posh we feel,
> United we all stand,
> We're telling you,
> Support the Blues,
> The best team in the land.
> Woah-oh!
> Peterborough, Peterborough, Peterborough la la la

## ⦚ NOBODY LIKES A LION

The most infamous anthem in British football is Millwall's chant 'No one Likes Us'. In the seventies, the club developed a reputation for hooliganism, although they were certainly not the only club with a violence problem as football disorder was rife throughout the UK.

However, Millwall fans felt they were unfairly targeted by the media and their fans made their feelings known with this chant to the tune of Rod Stewart's 'We Are Sailing' which has followed them around ever since – sadly, so has the hooligan reputation:

No one likes us, no one likes us,
No one likes us, we don't care,
We are Millwall, super Millwall
We are Millwall, from The Den

## ▦ COUNTY'S WHEELS COME OFF

Notts County's 'Wheelbarrow Song' was born out of a misheard chant
during a 1990 away game at Shrewsbury Town's wonderfully named Gay
Meadow. With County trailing 2-0 in the closing stages of the match, a small
group of frustrated fans had nothing better to do than make fun of a song
Shrewsbury were singing to the tune of 'On Top of Old Smoky'.

Whatever the real song was, County fans chanted what was to become the
'Wheelbarrow Song', the team scored two late goals to earn a point, the chant
caught on and the team didn't lose again that season.

In fact, County fans sang their new anthem all the way to Wembley, where
they defeated Tranmere to win promotion to the old Second Division – and
this is the song that carried them there and still carries them everywhere now:

I had a wheelbarrow, the wheel fell off,
I had a wheelbarrow, the wheel fell off,
I had a wheelbarrow, the wheel fell off,
I had a wheelbarrow, the wheel fell off...
County (clap clap clap)
County (clap clap clap)
County (clap clap clap)

## ▦ BARNET TWIST AND SHOUT

The reason is sometimes there is no reason. And that pretty much sums up
why Barnet fans sing 'Twist and Shout' during most matches. The Bees
actually perform a Beatles medley as they segue straight into the 'Hey Jude'
chorus too, although clearly this anthem is not unique to them as plenty of
other clubs use that for chants:

Shake it all baby now, (shake it all baby),
Twist and shout, (twist and shout),
Come on, come on baby now, (come on baby),
You know you work it all out, (work it all out),
You know you twist so good, (twist so good),
You know you twist so fine, (twist so fine),
Come on twist a little closer, (twist a little closer),
Let me know that you're mine, (know you're mine),
Woah!
La la la la-la la-la,
La-la la-la,
Barnet!

## ▦ NORTHAMPTON GO GREEN

Fans of Northampton Town enjoyed a purple patch in the mid-nineties and, as a result, a unique anthem was created. The Cobblers reached two successive play-off finals at Wembley, winning the first and losing the second, inspiring fans to dream up 'The Fields are Green'.

It's something of a mystery as to where the song was first aired, but it has certainly caught on over the years with supporters singing the following to the tune of 'Oh Christmas Tree':

The fields are green,
The skies are blue,
The river Nene goes winding through,
The market square is cobble stoned,
It shakes the old dears to the bones.
No finer town you'll ever see,
No finer town they'll ever be.
Big city lights don't bother me,
Northampton Town I'm proud to be.
The Cobblers! (clap clap clap)

# ▦ HARTLEPOOL'S BOYS' OWN

One of the more unusual anthems is Hartlepool's 'Two Little Boys'. The old tale of boys playing who go on to become soldiers at war was made famous by Rolf Harris, and Pools fans adopted the song in the early seventies. Several different sets of supporters claim to have been responsible for its regular airings at Hartlepool matches, but the north-east club's fans still sing it regardless of who was actually responsible. This is just part of the song which is usually sung, quite rapidly, in its entirety:

The tablecloth made a surprisingly good suit.

Two little boys had two little toys,
Each had a wooden horse,
Gaily they played each summer's day,
Warriors both, of course.

# ▦ SOUTHAMPTON'S GIFT FROM GOD

If your club nickname is The Saints, you're not going to have to look very far for an anthem. Southampton had a ready-made song waiting for them and they duly took it on, without changing a single word. Many other clubs sing their own versions of the song that was originally an American gospel hymn, but the south coast club's adherence to the original remains unique:

Oh when the Saints
Go marching in,
Oh when the Saints go marching in,
I want to be in that number,
When the Saints go marching in

# ▦ SKY BLUES SING TOGETHER

It's hard to imagine Arsène Wenger or Sir Alex Ferguson ever composing a chant for their respective clubs, but that's exactly what Coventry manager Jimmy Hill did in 1962. Together with director John Camkin, Hill, who also introduced the colour sky blue to the club and later became a TV football presenter, wrote an anthem to the tune of the 'Eton Boating Song' that's still popular with fans nearly 50 years later.

Jimmy Hill was lost in thought composing another song.

However, the lyrics have been updated to reflect that the club's rivals changed from the likes of Third Division Peterborough or Portsmouth in the sixties to Spurs and Chelsea, when they were in the top flight:

> Let's all sing together,
> Play up Sky Blues,
> While we sing together,
> We will never lose.
> Tottenham or Chelsea, United or anyone,
> They shan't defeat us,
> We'll fight till the game is won,
> City! (clap clap clap)
> City! (clap clap clap)

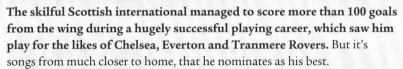

# PAT NEVIN

**The skilful Scottish international managed to score more than 100 goals from the wing during a hugely successful playing career, which saw him play for the likes of Chelsea, Everton and Tranmere Rovers.** But it's songs from much closer to home, that he nominates as his best.

'None of the ones about me really jump out, they were just the ones that everyone sings with my name in the end, like "There's only one Pat Nevin".

'Everyone talks about "You'll Never Walk Alone" which is very moving but there are other anthems and my team Hibernian sing "Sunshine on Leith" on special occasions. I remember covering a match in which Hibs were playing in the Scottish League Cup final a few years back. They hadn't won anything for a long time. I was in the studio with Dougie Donnelly after the game. I was aware as a Hibee that they were going to start singing it and I did not want to talk over it. So I said to Dougie "when they start singing that song, I'm not talking".

'Dougie gave me a kind of look as I heard the strains of it start up and I gave him a look back and he just said: "Let's go outside and enjoy the moment". I don't think the people producing the show were aware of just how beautiful a moment that was going to be – and it was. John Collins, the manager and big Hibee had just lost his dad, so it was a really great moment.

'I've always liked quick-fire chants between fans. The most recent example of hearing anything like that was at Hibs when Hearts fans were singing: "All the Hibees are gay!" [to "Seven Nation Army"]. But at the times the Hearts players were having problems getting paid by the club, so the Hibs fans chanted back: "All the Hibees got paid!"

'I thought that was a very good and quick reaction.'

Nevin was so good he was often forced to play on one foot.

# 11

# THE CHANTS DIRECTORY

This book would not be complete without mentioning the basic songs that make up the large majority of terrace noise every week. While we all have many specific chants for certain occasions, we also sing the same songs, whether they be about the referee, opposition fans or our teams. This chapter is for those chants that we take for granted – the songs that make up the soundtrack of our Saturdays and they're presented here in dictionary format for easy reference.

### 'Are you [insert poor team or rivals] in disguise?'

Sung to the tune of 'Bread of Heaven', fans of a team in the ascendancy will normally chant this at their opponents to further rub their noses in it and make them wish they'd done that urgent DIY after all.

### '[insert manager and team colours]'s army!'

Sung as a chant with no tune to demonstrate support for the team and manager, fans will usually begin clapping along to this chant and attempt to keep it going for far longer than is strictly necessary. Usually sung by fans of a team that's winning or during a boring passage of play.

### 'Can we play you every week?'

Another cruel song to the tune of 'Bread of Heaven' chanted by fans of a winning team to their opponents to suggest an unlikely regular fixture in the belief their team would win every time – even though this would actually contravene the rules and notion of league football.

### 'Come on [insert team name]'

An unoriginal yet occasionally inspiring chant in which fans sing their team's name after 'Come on' to offer them vocal backing. Usually chanted following the award of a corner or a free kick in a dangerous position.

### 'E-I-E-I-E-I-O, up the Football League we go...'

A predominantly northern chant, sung by fans of teams who are in the promotion places, or very close to them, demonstrating the belief that they will indeed win promotion. The initial letters are usually sung the loudest with outstretched arms before mumbling as quickly through the rest of the song as possible in order to be able to reach the part where the letters can be shouted again.

### 'England's number one'

An optimistic chant sung by fans about their goalkeepers after they've pulled off a spectacular save, suggesting they should wear the England team's goalkeeping shirt. Plausible in the Premier League but less likely in the Blue Square Premier.

### '[insert manager's name] give us a wave'

Normally sung when a team is winning handsomely, as fans invite their manager to join in the fun atmosphere by offering them a wave. Always followed by a cheer when the manager obliges and occasionally followed by a boo when he does not.

### 'Going down'

Straight and to the point, this chant (to 'Stars and Stripes Forever') is directed at the fans of a team that is in danger of being relegated – or has already been relegated. Usually, it's not sung as a warning as the recipient fans will be well aware of their club's perilous plight.

### 'Here we go'

An eighties chant also sung to American marching band tune 'Stars and Stripes Forever' by fans to lift their team or to celebrate following a goal. Dropped like a stone in the nineties once senses of humour became more widespread.

### 'Is that all you bring away?'

Chanted by home fans (to 'Bread of Heaven') to a set of travelling fans who have more empty seats around them than occupied ones. Occasionally used ironically to confuse away fans who have taken their full allocation of tickets.

### 'It's just like watching The Bill'

A contemporary chant playing on Barnsley's 'Watching Brazil' that's sung by fans at any match with a large police presence.

### 'Let him die'

Particularly cruel and unpleasant chant sung by fans (to 'Stars and Stripes Forever') wishing a permanent deceasing of whichever opposition player happens to be lying injured on the pitch at the time.

### 'Let's all have a disco'

An eighties chant sung by fans looking for an excuse to jump up and down and pretend they're at a discotheque for no other reason than boredom as all football was, of course, extremely dull until the Premier League was invented.

### 'Let's go fucking mental'

Another eighties chant with similar origins to 'Let's all have a disco'. Both were sung to the 'Conga' tune.

### 'Let's pretend we've scored a goal'

A chant rich in irony usually sung (to 'Bread of Heaven') by fans of a team who are being heavily beaten 'to-nil', trying to keep their spirits up by imagining a goal. Normally followed by a faux celebration as wild as that of a promotion-winning goal.

### 'My old man'

A supremely offensive chant sung by fans about their main rivals to the tune of music hall favourite 'My Old Man (said follow the van)'. In this case, the parent in question suggests his son should become a supporter of the rival team only for the offspring in question to reply with a 'go forth and multiply, testicles, you're a female sexual organ'.

### 'OFF! OFF! OFF!'

Chanted by fans of a team whose player has been badly fouled in an attempt to persuade the referee to issue the culprit with a red card. Occasionally successful so always worth a try.

### 'Oh [insert city name] is full of shit'

Fans will sing this about a rival or neighbouring town or city usually straight after singing about how wonderful their own town or city is (see below). They describe the offending place as 'full of shit, shit and more shit' even though the original 'shit' would have sufficed.

### 'Oh [insert city name] is wonderful'

Sung by fans (to 'Oh When the Saints') to marvel at the attractions on offer in their town or city. The reasons given are usually threefold. One, it contains ladies' breasts. Two, it contains ladies' sexual reproductive organs. Three, it contains the team they support.

### 'Ole'

Shouted as one by fans when their team manage to string a succession of passes together. Deriving from South America, each time a pass is completed the fans will yell their approval with 'Ole' until an opposition player touches the ball at which point everyone has to boo.

### 'One [insert name], there's only one [insert name]'

Sung to the tune of 'Guantanamera' this is the easiest form of hero-worshipping a favourite player by simply inserting his name in the right places. Usually chanted if that player has scored a goal, gone on a mazy, dribbling run or made a great save (but never all three).

### 'One-nil'

In the days before 'Go West' this was chanted by fans of a team that had opened the scoring, to the tune of 'Amazing Grace'. Yes kids, it really happened.

### 'One-nil to the [insert team name]'

Originally sung by Arsenal to 'Go West' (a hit in 1979 for the Village People, below), now used everywhere by fans of teams who have opened the scoring to remind their opponents that they're losing. Particularly useful in lower division grounds without scoreboards.

The Arsenal Christmas party was certain to hit the headlines.

### '[insert team name] reject'

Usually sung by fans to a former player who has returned to play against his old club after being moved on. Occasionally, it will be chanted ironically at a former player who decided to leave and went on to even greater success and clearly wasn't a 'reject'.

## 'Sacked in the morning'

Gleefully chanted by fans towards the manager of the team they're beating (to 'Guantanamera') without a second thought that they're informing him that he's unlikely to be able to provide for his family following the match.

## 'Said Bertie Mee to Bill Shankly...'

A very old chant in which fans imagine a conversation between the two great managers (to the tune of 'Tom Hark'). It goes like this: 'Have you heard of the North Bank, Highbury?' 'No, I don't think so' and ends with 'But I've heard of the...' at which point the fans insert the name of their particular stand or hooligan firm to prove how fearsome they are.

## 'Shall we score a goal for you?'

Usually sung by fans of a team who are winning by a considerable margin (at least three goals) to taunt their opposite numbers. There are, as yet, no recorded instances of any of these fans entering the field of play to pull a goal back on behalf of the opposition.

## 'Shall we sing a song for you?'

Sung by one set of boisterous fans (to 'Bread of Heaven') to their quieter opposite numbers to demonstrate how poor their support has been. The fans never actually sing one of their opponents' songs, but will often sing one of their own straight away. See also 'Your support is fucking shit'.

## 'She fell over'

A mocking chant sung by fans about an opposition player who is writhing on the floor in agony. The use of the female pronoun was devised to add to the humour.

## 'Shit ground, no fans'

Sung by away fans when visiting a below-standard and scarcely populated venue to watch their team (to 'Westminster Chimes'). Also sang ironically by fans of lower division teams when visiting top class Premier League stadiums which are full to capacity.

### 'Sing when you're winning'

Usually sung in frustration (to 'Guantanamera') by away fans who have spent most of the match chanting for their team in an otherwise quiet ground only for the home team to score and their fans to suddenly burst into song.

### 'Sing your hearts out for the lads'

Passionate, raw and 'Ronseal' style song, which does exactly what it says on the tin. Fans that sing this, to the tune of 'Bread of Heaven' are actually fulfilling the message of their song. See also 'We'll support you ever more'

### 'Singing the Blues'

Sung by fans about their rivals, this was first chanted by Bristol Rovers about City but is now widely used as supporters sing about never being happier than when their team win and their rivals lose, despite everything we're told about gloating being unbecoming.

### 'Sit down, shut up'

A product of the all-seater stadium environment in which football is now played, this chant (to the 'Westminster Chimes') is usually heard by fans who have had just about enough of the noise made by their opposite numbers. Also heard when one team's fans think they've scored only to realise the goal has been ruled out – the other set of fans will then invite them to return to their seats. See also 'You thought you had scored'

### 'Stand up if you hate [insert team]'

Used by fans of one team to all declare their united hatred of their biggest rivals, sung to the tune of 'Go West' preferably with arms spread out wide or planted above head. Any fan remaining seated risks being labelled a fan of said hated team.

### 'Stand up if you love [insert team]'

Used by fans of a team to all declare their united love for that team, sung to the tune of 'Go West' preferably with arms spread out wide or planted above head. Any fan remaining seated also risks being labelled a fan of their biggest rivals.

### 'The Football League is upside-down'

An oldie but goodie in which fans of a team in desperate trouble at the bottom of a division will pretend they're really fighting for promotion (to 'Oh When the Saints'). Guaranteed to raise a chuckle during hard times before the immediate realisation of doom sets in again.

### The Great Escape

A rare example of a 'chant' almost totally without words as fans sing the theme tune from the film and end by yelling their own team's name before starting all over again. First heard at the 1998 World Cup, and aided and abetted by the England band ever since.

Despite an audience of zero, the band played on regardless.

### 'The referee's a wanker'

Chanted by any set of fans who feel wronged by an official's decision, and who will often have spittle seen on their lips while shouting the words. The chant has nothing to do with the actual masturbatory habits of the official, as we all know that everyone does it.

### '[insert name] till I die'

Sung to the tune of old religious song 'I'm H A P P Y', this is the ultimate pledge of allegiance to one club by fans. Usually chanted with arms raised and wide apart for added emphasis just in case 'I know I am, I'm sure I am' wasn't enough.

### 'Two-nil and you fucked it up'

Occasionally starting with three or four-nil, this chant (to 'Go West') is sung by fans of a team who have launched an unlikely comeback (to either draw level or take the lead) to taunt rival supporters about how their team failed to make the most of their advantage.

### 'Vindaloo song'

A chant that became popular following the 1998 World Cup, consisting of many 'ders' followed by a shouting of the particular team's name. Usually sung out of tune for maximum impact.

### 'We're going to win 5-4'

An ironic chant sung (to 'Blue Moon') by fans of a team on the wrong end of a drubbing who try to make themselves feel better by pretending their team is going to launch an extraordinary comeback. Normally sung in the closing stages of a match to ratchet up the irony factor.

### 'We're on the march with [insert manager]'s army...'

An old-fashioned chant sung by supporters of teams who have advanced sufficiently far enough in a cup competition for them to believe they're on their way to Wembley. They also believe that they will be shaking things up by winning said cup, possibly a reference to champagne.

### 'We can see you sneaking out'

'Bread of Heaven' is the tune for this song, which is chanted by fans of a team who are in an unassailable position towards their opposite numbers who are heading for the exits in the closing minutes of the match, proving there are no hiding places on the pitch – or in the stands.

### 'We'll support you ever more'

An old-fashioned loyalty song sung to 'Bread of Heaven'. See 'Sing your hearts out for the lads'.

## 'We love you [insert team], we do'

An old-fashioned but ever-popular chant in which fans display devotion to their team. Most often heard at the end of a game which has been won or, possibly, at the end of a cup-tie in which a lower division team has played well but lost to higher-ranked opponents. At this point, the lower-placed team's fans feel the need to remind the players that they're loved, even in defeat.

## 'We shall not be moved'

A chant sung by many clubs with a variety of reasons for the aforementioned stubbornness. Sometimes, the fans won't be moved because they're going to win a league or cup while others won't leave their spot because they're intending to avoid relegation.

## 'When I was just a little boy...'

Sung by fans about their rivals, this chant involves singing the first two lines of 'Que Sera, Sera' (originally performed by Doris Day, below) then imagining asking one's mother which of two rival teams should be supported only for this imaginary parent to offer the extremely unlikely parental advice of taking a gun and shooting the enemy team.

## 'Where were you when you were shit?'

A modern-day phenomenon chanted at fans of clubs which have risen from relative obscurity thanks to a wealthy benefactor, and subsequently saw attendances double because of their new-found success. Always chanted with a point to the section of the crowd who look most suspiciously like consumers of prawn sandwiches.

Unfortunately, the powersuit's trousers hadn't arrived in the post.

### 'Who are ya?'

No tune, but a war cry of a chant screamed at opposing fans normally by supporters of a team who have just scored. Usually sung while pointing at the group of fans. Occasionally, this is chanted ironically at an opposition player who, in fact, everyone chanting would actually know.

### 'Who ate all the pies?'

Sung to the tune of 'Knees Up Mother Brown'. See 'You fast bastard!' for examples of when and how it's used.

### 'Who the fucking hell are you?'

See 'Who Are Ya?'

### 'Wooooooooaaaaaaaah! You're shit, aaaaaaaaaaaaaaaaaaaaaaaaah'

An eighties classic, still heard at some lower league grounds today, chanted by fans behind the goal just before a goalkeeper is about take a goal kick. Soon after the keeper places the ball on the six-yard line, the fans will begin with 'Wooooooah' and one hundredth of a second before contact between the keeper's boot and the ball, the rest of the chant will be completed in an (mostly vain) attempt to put him off.

### 'You all support [insert team]'

A lower league favourite as visiting fans tease their hosts (to 'Blue Moon') by suggesting their real loyalties lie with the much bigger club up the road. Usually results in home fans laughing it off or being genuinely wound up to the point of police intervention.

### 'You fat bastard!'

A combined chant and point in the direction of an opposition player who seems to be carrying an extra few pounds. Also chanted at overweight opposition fans who can be spotted from a distance, and occasionally at lardy looking physios who waddle on to the pitch to treat injured players.

### 'You only came to see the [insert team]'

Chanted by visiting fans of so-called big teams to home supporters (to 'Guantanamera') when they discover a full house awaiting them at grounds which are never normally sold out. Also sung ironically by fans of small clubs playing at a bigger club's ground in a cup-tie.

### 'You'll never beat [insert player's name]'

When a goalkeeper makes a decent stop or a hard-nut defender makes a desperate goal-saving tackle, fans will sing this chant despite the obvious fact that those players *have* been beaten time and again, otherwise all records for never conceding a goal would have been broken.

### '[insert the competition] – You're having a laugh!'

Sung (to the tune of 'Tom Hark') by fans of one team, to tease their opponents about their aspirations to win a certain competition or their very presence in a particular tournament. For example, a top-flight team being beaten by a lower division side in the FA Cup, would often hear 'Premier League, you're having a laugh!' sung at them.

### 'You're not fit to referee'

Chanted by fans who feel wronged by an entire set of decisions from the official. Usually sung after 'The referee's a wanker' to express further dissatisfaction with the official, to the tune of 'Bread of Heaven'.

### 'You're not fit to wear the shirt'

A chant of anger (to 'Bread of Heaven') directed by fans towards their own players normally sung during a particularly incompetent performance which has most supporters telling their neighbours 'this is the last time I waste my money on this lot' before returning for more a fortnight later.

### 'You're not very good!'

Chanted by fans towards an opposition player, who has not performed to the standards expected of a professional footballer. Sung to the tune of 'Knees Up Mother Brown' usually while pointing at the culprit, lest there be any misunderstanding about who's being humiliated.

### 'You're shit and you know you are!'

The modern version of 'You're so shit it's unbelievable' sung by fans to the tune of 'Go West' to a poorly performing opponent or to a set of opposition fans who are watching their team being beaten. Includes obligatory pointing at target(s) throughout.

### 'You're so shit it's unbelievable'

An old-fashioned chant, the pre-cursor to 'You're shit and you know you are', sung by fans to an opposition player who has belied his professionalism to come up with something that you would expect to see on a park pitch on a Sunday morning.

### 'You're supposed to be at home'

A staple for away fans whose team are in the ascendancy, sung to the tune of 'Bread of Heaven', to increase the suffering of home supporters. A point of the finger towards the nearest home fans coincides with the singing of the word 'You're'.

### 'Your support is fucking shit'

Chanted by one set of fans to another to inform them of their wholly inadequate backing for their team – especially compared to their own which is, of course, far superior. Another 'Bread of Heaven' staple.

### 'You're gonna get your fucking heads kicked in'

Seventies war cry sung by one set of fans to another to serve notice of the violence that was scheduled to take place on their heads following the match.

The policemen always cuddled up to their suspects.

### 'You'll never reach the station'
Seventies number sung by home fans to warn their visitors that there was absolutely no likelihood whatsoever of them completing their journeys home due to the fatal violence that was awaiting them following the game.

### 'You're not singing anymore'
One of the most popular chants in British football usually sung by a set of fans celebrating a goal who then turn to the opposition fans to taunt them. Always chanted to 'Bread of Heaven' with a finger pointing rudely at the other supporters on the word 'You're'.

### 'You thought you had scored, you were wrong'
An older chant sung by fans to opponents who have celebrated an offside goal, believing it would count, only to then notice the linesman's flag. See also 'Sit down, shut up'.

### 'You've only got one song'
Sung to opposition fans who have kept singing the same chant throughout a match with no variation and no sign of a songbook. Usually followed by the opposition singing a different song.

# MICK QUINN

**A striker straight out of the old school, Mick Quinn was prolific
wherever he played, notching more than 200 goals in a fabulous career.**
The fans took to Quinn wherever he went as his stocky build and eye for goal
meant he was an obvious subject of chants from the terraces.

'I used to laugh so much about those songs,' he recalls. 'Portsmouth fans
used to sing this one at home matches [to the tune of Quartermaster's Store']:

> He's fat, he's round,
> He's worth a million pound,
> Micky Quinn, Micky Quinn!

Meanwhile, the opposition fans would normally sing:

> He's fat, he's round,
> His arse is on the ground,
> Micky Quinn, Micky Quinn!

'But my favourite chant was when I played for Newcastle. And that's when
this song was born [to 'The Mighty Quinn']:

> Come on without,
> Come on within,
> You ain't seen nothing
> Like the mighty Quinn

'The feeling is amazing when you hear the fans singing
to you. To me, it was an extension of being on the Kop
when I used to watch Liverpool and sing songs to Keegan
and Dalglish.'

Quinny had just heard about the 'Buy one get one free' deal at the pie stall.

# ▥ ACKNOWLEDGEMENTS

The following people all play or played football and deemed me worthy of a quick chat about their favourite chant. I am grateful to them all: Alan Brazil, Jimmy Bullard, Tony Cascarino, Stan Collymore, Jason Cundy, Andy Gray, Matt Holland, Ray Houghton, Chris Kamara, Pat Nevin, Alvin Martin and Mick Quinn.

The following people supplied me with chants or helped me find out more about a chant. They were all really nice too: Elinor Block, Bill Borrows, Pete Boyle, Simon Burnton, Sam Coare, John Cooper, Dave the Latics fan, Andrew Dickens, Joe Ellison, Peter Etherington, Jimi Famurewa, Julian Flanders, Jack Gaughan, Marc Higginson, Mike Jenkins (*Watch the Bluebirds Fly*), Pat Llanwarne, Peps Mall, James McMahon, Damian Mannion, Chris Mendes, Joseph Miller, Josh Milligan, Paul (*Three Lions and a Robin*), Joel Naftalin, Jonathan Pile, Josh Portnoi, Doron Rosenfeld, David Ross, Craig Stevens, Laurie Sudwarts, Ron Tabbouche, Michael Teichner, Alex Walker (ltlf.co.uk), Steve Welch and Gareth Willsher.

The following people spoke to me about chanting and were very clever: Professor Mike Weed (Kent University) and John Williams (Leicester University).

The following people all wore smart clothes and worked behind the scenes to help make this book a reality: Adam Bullock, Jonathan Conway, Moz Dee, Ian Marshall, Anna Robinson, Rory Scarfe and Scott Taunton.

The following people know me very well but didn't see me for a few months while I was writing this book. I love them: Victoria and Jake.

The following season did not disappoint with its habitual lack of sunshine, therefore not tempting me away from my desk: English summer.

The publishers would like to thank the following for supplying the photographs used in this book:
**Action Images** pages 23, 27, 76, 159; **Getty Images** pages 8, 29, 39, 43, 54, 63, 70, 88, 91, 93, 98, 100, 101, 105, 108, 116, 131, 139, 143, 147, 152, 164, 167, 172 and **PA Photos** pages 10, 14, 18, 33, 47, 51, 52, 60, 65, 67, 78, 83, 95, 110, 117, 119, 124, 128, 134, 136, 157, 158, 169, 174. The chapter title artwork was taken from an image supplied by istockphoto.com/nico_blue

# ▥ DEDICATION

**For Ma and Pa**

The following resources were used in the research and writing of this book:

**thesun.co.uk**
**mirrorfootball.co.uk**
**dailystar.co.uk**
**independent.co.uk**
**thetimes.co.uk**
**telegraph.co.uk**
**guardian.co.uk**
**dailymail.co.uk**
**express.co.uk**
**bbc.co.uk**
**youtube.com**
**fanchants.com**
**wikipedia.com**
**soccerbase.com**
**thisisleicestershire.co.uk**
**thisisbristol.co.uk**
**canaries.co.uk**
**ccfc.co.uk**
**nottscountyfc.co.uk**
**portsmouthfc.co.uk**
**Lyrics by The Proclaimers**